THE WILD WEEKEND DIET

THE ·WILD WEEKEND· DIET

Lois Lindauer

of The Diet Workshop

PIATKUS

THE DIET WORKSHOP®, ®, and Flexi-Diet® are registered trademarks, and Wild Weekend Diet® is a trademark of The Diet Workshop, Inc., Brookline, Massachusetts.

© 1985 Lois Lindauer

First published in Great Britain
in 1986 by Judy Piatkus (Publishers) Limited,
5 Windmill Street, London W1P 1HS

British Library Cataloguing in Publication Data
Lindauer, Lois
  The wild weekend diet.
  1. Reducing diets   2. Physical fitness
  I. Title
  613.2'5   RM222.2

  ISBN 0–86188–397–7

Text anglicised by Miranda Hall
Designed by Paul Saunders

Phototypeset by D. P. Media Limited, Hitchin, Hertfordshire
Printed and bound by Mackays of Chatham Limited, Chatham, Kent

Contents

Acknowledgements 7

Conversion Tables 8

Introduction 9

CHAPTER 1
Thank God It's Friday! 11

CHAPTER 2
The Wild Weekend Diet 18

CHAPTER 3
Off for the Weekend 23

CHAPTER 4
Weekday Slimdown Plan 40

CHAPTER 5
Eating Out on a Wild Weekend 80

CHAPTER 6
Holidays and Special Occasions 106

CHAPTER 7
Appetisers and Accompaniments 117

CHAPTER 8
Main Courses, Vegetables and Fruits 132

CHAPTER 9
Desserts, Dairy and Beverages 149

CHAPTER 10
Dieting Seven Days a Week: The Flexi-Diet 161

CHAPTER 11
The Last Ten Pounds plus Best Diet Tips   180

CHAPTER 12
Maintenance and a New Beginning   198

ACKNOWLEDGEMENTS

To Kathy Ettinger, who researched painstakingly, to Donna Roazen, who commented and suggested carefully, and to Laura Warren, who picked up the pieces, I am grateful.

•

I should also like to thank nutrition expert and cookery writer Miranda Hall for her excellent work in adapting this book for the British market.

Conversion Tables

WEIGHT	
oz	g
½	12
⅔	18
¾	20
1	25
2	50
3	80
3½	100
4	115
5	140
6	170
7	200
8	225
9	250
10	280
11	325
12	350
14	400
16	450
1½ lb	675
2 lb (approx)	1 kg

CAPACITY		
pints	fl oz	ml
¼	5	150
½	10	300
¾	15	425
1	20	600
1 mug	8	225
1 wine glass	4	115

OVEN TEMPERATURE		
300°F	150°C	mark 2
325°F	160°C	mark 3
350°F	180°C	mark 4
375°F	190°C	mark 5
400°F	200°C	mark 6
425°F	210°C	mark 7

INTRODUCTION

This book is dedicated to the understanding that for most people, the most consistent pleasure in their lives is food. Think about it . . . how many people, activities, or possessions do you find more exciting than food?

Food is a reliable comfort. Food is easy to find and eating is easy to do. The process is almost automatic; it's the button we push for solace, for relief of boredom, for joy, for sociability, and – oh, yes – for hunger.

Given a choice of being fat or thin, you'd probably opt for thin. It's when you're given a choice between thin and a chocolate cream cake that the choosing gets hard! To reconcile the excitement of eating to the visual image you'd like for yourself is not simple. Or easy. It's the ever-present battle between long-term goals versus short-term gratification.

It's easy to fail on a diet. Everybody does at some time or other. Food pushers everywhere love a diet failure. They stand ready and willing to remind others that it's 'only normal' to forget one's resolves. Watching you fall off the diet wagon relieves their guilt about their own failure.

You've probably experienced being fat and thin in your life and know that thin is better. When you know that:

- Thin is better than beer at a football game.
- Thin is better than a Mars bar mid-morning.
- Thin is better than a choc-ice at the cinema.
- Thin is better than a cream doughnut or a sticky bun.
- Thin is better than a black cherry cheesecake.
- Thin is better than McDonald's burgers.
- Thin is better than fish and chips on Friday.
- Thin is best!

Then you know you *can* be thin!

If any of the above activities and/or foods especially speak to you, be of good cheer: you need not banish them from your life forever. What you must do is acknowledge the reality that you can't have everything you want all of the time. You've got to make choices. Every day. Every meal. And you can elect to enjoy your special foods. But not all the time.

And that's what this book is about.

Lois Lindauer

· CHAPTER ONE ·

THANK GOD IT'S FRIDAY!

In the best of all possible diet worlds there would be no weekends. Without the temptation of Saturdays and Sundays most of us would stay with a diet for seven days a week, lose our weight, and get thin.

Unfortunately real life is not like that. Most people find it hard to diet at the weekends. If you eat at a friend's or at a relative's house, you may have no choices in what you eat. If you eat in a restaurant, you probably have too many choices. If you stay at home, you may feel lonely or bored, and, possibly, sorry for yourself – feelings that rank high among diet killers.

Whatever the reason, whatever the season, there is no doubt that Saturday night is the hungriest night of the week. The iron resolve you made on Monday crumbles to sawdust on Saturday when the siren sings ever so sweetly of exotic cocktails, lasagna or lemon meringue pie.

At last here is a diet that meets the Saturday night challenge head-on. It is called The Wild Weekend Diet, and with it you will scale weekend hurdles, steer effortlessly through the weekend obstacle course, and come to a triumphant rest at your weight goal.

So what makes a weekend wild?

Well, dieter, if you can eat pizza or steak and kidney pie or cherry cheesecake and still lose weight, that, to me, is wild.

On The Wild Weekend Diet your need to be sociable and to enjoy your food on Saturday night is recognised and taken care of, whether you eat in or out. Whatever the circumstance, you'll be eating food you love, food that satisfies heart and soul as well as the stomach.

On The Wild Weekend Diet you can have your cake, eat it, and still lose weight!

How The Wild Weekend Diet was created

The Diet Workshop was formed in 1965 in the United States. Over the years it has learned from hundreds of thousands of dieters that people will succeed on a diet and reach goal weight only if they feel satisfied. It is our experience that the dieter who feels deprived is the dieter who falls off the wagon. After that, Humpty Dumpty takes over and the diet never gets back together again. We also found that the people who enjoy what they're eating can stay on a diet indefinitely and that they do get thin!

Many dieters were at first sceptical when encouraged to take the weekend off their strict diets, but those who did found that they were able to stick to them much longer. These dieters had a greater chance of being successful in achieving their weight loss goals. Many people can only sustain the discipline of sticking to a strict diet for short periods at a time. The promise of a liberated diet at the weekend was what they needed if they were to have long-term success. It was, therefore, using this understanding of the people who diet that The Wild Weekend Diet was developed.

Satisfied that we had a formula that everyone could follow with successful results, The Diet Workshop was ready to share this new and revolutionary way to lose weight with dieters in America and around the world.

How the diet works

As you probably know, most recommended diets provide about 1,200 calories a day for women and 1,500 for men. These calories are portioned out over three meals and snacks, each meal containing protein, such as fish, chicken, meat, cheese or eggs, and a carbohydrate, such as bread, potato, rice or starchy vegetables. Other vegetables, fruits and milk each day are also part of these eating plans.

The arithmetic is simple: 1,200 calories per day for women, 1,500 calories per day for men, when multiplied by the seven days of the week gives us a total of 8,400 calories per week for women and 10,500 calories for men.

Instead of portioning the calories out evenly during the week, The Wild Weekend Diet allows approximately half of the week's calories from Monday through to Friday and the remaining calories on the two weekend days.

The Wild Weekend Diet is a well balanced diet, and you will still control your weekly amount of food, but you eat sparingly during the week so that you can eat your favourite foods at the weekend.

The mid-week plan

From Monday to Friday, the diet you follow is structured, strict and simple (see Chapter 4). Because of this simplicity you will not have to count calories; that has been done for you. Each day that you follow this weekday plan, you save hundreds of calories, which you can then spend as you choose over the weekend. From apple pie to zabaglione, all foods are available for your choosing. And, most important, at the end of each and every week you lose weight.

The calorie count

The calories in lettuce count in exactly the same way as the calories in lasagna. It will not, however, astonish you to hear that there are many more calories in lasagna.

The point of this information is to let you know that your body can burn up only a limited number of calories each day. If you exceed your body's ability to burn up calories in the food you eat, these calories accumulate in your body as fat. If you eat less than your calorie burn-up rate, you will burn up your body fat and lose weight.

The Wild Weekend Diet is planned so that over the seven

days of the week, your total calorie intake is below your body's calorie maintenance level. Therefore, you create a calorie deficit and lose weight.

As on other balanced eating plans, weight loss for the first week of dieting is about 3 to 5 pounds (1.4 to 2.25 kg) for women, 4 to 7 pounds (1.8 to 3.2 kg) for men. On each succeeding week, weight loss averages out to about half the amount lost in week one. So, if you have 25 pounds (11.3 kg) to lose and you're a woman, it will take you about three months of healthy Wild Weekend dieting for you to reach your goal.

There may come a time, of course, when you are faced by that old diet bugbear – plateau. You lose weight very nicely for a time and then you get stuck on one level – the plateau – and you just can't seem to drop below it. When you reach this stubborn level remember our promise to you: if you keep on dieting you'll keep on losing. The weight loss may not show up on the scales exactly at the moment you want and/or expect it to, but you will get the result you're looking for if you are confident about what you're doing and you stay with it.

We deal with that special plateau, the one that occurs when you're about 10 pounds (4.5 kg) from your goal and most anxious to lose weight, in Chapter 11, The Last Ten Pounds plus Best Diet Tips. The suggestions there will work well any time you're going through a plateau during your weight-loss process and want quick results.

The Wild Weekend bank account

The Wild Weekend Diet works just like your bank account. Consider your calorie allotment as your salary. If you spend in money (or use up in calories) more than you put into your bank account (or yourself) you will end up with a deficit. Your bank manager may not like to see you with an overdraft, but deficit budgeting with calories is what successful slimming is all about.

By only eating 8,400 calories as a woman or 10,500 as a man, your income (or intake) will be less than you are withdrawing to use in energy through the week. To compensate for this overdraft, your body will have to call on your other reserves (your body fat) and use this to settle your debt.

As long as your income or intake in calories over the whole week is not exceeded, it will not matter which day of the week these are banked. By restricting yourself Monday to Friday you can afford to be generous and enjoy your Wild Weekend splurge.

No-think diet

Our experience has told us that counting calories is not only dismal drudgery but also highly inaccurate. This probably doesn't astonish you. The Wild Weekend Diet assesses the calories for you, whether those calories are in a casserole dish or in a grilled steak. The assessment process gives you your best chance for success.

The calorie information is given to you in a very simple way. Each food has been assigned a unit value. You will add Wild Weekend Units (WWUs) as you choose and control the foods you eat on your Wild Weekend Diet.

Being thin for ever

The Wild Weekend Diet is more than just a diet. It is a whole concept in eating and an information system by which you can regulate your weight in a healthy, happy and successful way for the rest of your life.

By adopting the eating patterns and using the knowledge you acquire as you lose weight, you are also learning how to maintain that weight loss. As you experiment with and practise the principles of The Wild Weekend Diet you are at the same time mastering the system that will keep you thin for ever.

Healthy eating

Since we recommend The Wild Weekend Diet as a lifetime eating guide, you need to know how it relates to your body's nutritional needs.

Although our bodies have different requirements, there are common needs we share. These needs, Recommended Daily Allowances, have been established by the Food and Nutrition Board of the National Academy of Science in the United States and the Ministry of Agriculture, Fisheries and Food in the United Kingdom.

Many people believe that these requirements are difficult to obtain from our nutrient-depleted soil and take vitamins and minerals to supplement their food intake. Many people also believe that these requirements are difficult to obtain from a slimming diet. Great care has been taken to ensure that this diet meets these requirements as closely as possible by keeping processed foods to a minimum and encouraging a wide range of fruit and vegetables. Nevertheless, the diet will be low in Vitamin D, and extra B vitamins may help with the conversion of food to energy instead of fat. Therefore, although you will be eating a healthy diet, we recommend a food supplement in the form of good vitamin and mineral tablets.

That is your second step to good health. The *first* step to good health is eating a well-balanced diet, and The Wild Weekend Diet is such a diet.

Well-balanced diet

It is essential to your body's good functioning that, in addition to vitamins and nutrients, you eat daily amounts of protein, carbohydrates and fats. A well-balanced diet includes these nutrients at each meal.

Protein is a body builder. It provides the amino acids necessary to produce cells for growth, maintenance and repair of tissue. Amino acids are also necessary to produce enzymes and antibodies. Enzymes regulate your body processes. Antibodies fight infection and disease. Protein also helps to maintain a high metabolic rate, the rate at which the body burns up fat. On The Wild Weekend Diet you will be dining on protein when you eat fish, meat, poultry, cheese and eggs.

The carbohydrates you eat give you energy and help you to think. You will be eating carbohydrates at each meal when you eat breakfast cereal, bread, rice, fruits and vegetables. They are an important part of your healthy diet and should not be considered simply as being 'fattening'.

Fibre is now considered a vital part of the diet, encouraging the speedy elimination of waste products to keep you 'regular'. This will affect your long-term good health and your short-term sense of well-being. For this reason only whole grain foods are included on your mid-week diet: whole grain breakfast cereal, wholemeal bread, brown rice, jacket potatoes plus a variety of fruit and vegetables.

Fats provide concentrated energy and are therefore high in calories. Some fat is essential in the diet, but any diet high in animal fats – and cholesterol – is not considered good for health. For this reason the number of eggs is limited, lean poultry is given largely in preference to red meat, low fat cheese is mainly recommended, but oily fish included occasionally for its useful contribution to good health.

If any variations are made to the recommended diet they must be chosen with great care to ensure that they provide all the essential vitamins and minerals as well as similar food value. Those whose needs are special – children, teenagers and pregnant women – will find additional advice on pages 177 and 178.

· CHAPTER TWO ·

THE WILD WEEKEND DIET

On The Wild Weekend Diet, as with all other eating plans, there are certain guidelines to follow. The Wild Weekend Diet works because you apportion your calories in a very unique way. You eat fewer calories during the week and spend those 'saved' calories at the weekend when you want them the most. On The Wild Weekend Diet you enjoy your Saturday nights just as you did in your pre-diet days. So, whether it's your birthday or a holiday, or simply because you want a change, you will be eating along with the rest of your friends even though you are on a weight-loss programme.

Weekend Slimdown Plan and Wild Weekend Units

The Wild Weekday Diet is really two diets in one. The first diet is followed during the week – Monday to Friday – while the second is reserved for the weekend.

The mid-week diet is called the Weekday Slimdown Plan (WSP). The WSP offers you a variety of menus to follow each weekday, each of which provides calories to bank away for the weekend spending spree. The Weekday Slimdown Plan is a diet structured to guarantee your success. It dictates which food and how much you will eat at each meal.

You are probably already more interested in your weekend eating and how the diet works, as your weekends are going to sustain you through the disciplined weeks ahead. For starters, here is some information on Wild Weekend Units (WWUs).

Each of you has a Wild Weekend Unit allowance, which controls what and how much you eat during the Wild Weekend. Women are permitted a total of 35 WWUs, and men are allowed 44. These WWUs are eaten exclusively on Saturday night and for Sunday lunch.

Women can eat 22 WWUs for dinner on Saturday night and 13 WWUs for Sunday lunch while men can eat 29 WWUs on Saturday night and 15 WWUs for Sunday lunch.

What is a Wild Weekend Unit?

One Wild Weekend Unit averages no more than 75 calories. In fact, a food item that has been designed as 1 WWU may contain as few as 25 calories or it may contain as many as 75 calories. For you, though, it will always be 1 WWU.

You will find that we have listed dozens of popular foods and assigned WWUs to them. If your favourite is an ethnic dish or a fast-food item, you'll probably find it on our list. And just in case it's not there, we show you how to create your own WWU lists (see page 117). So whether you are cooking a special meal at home, dining at friends', eating at your local curry house or at the Ritz you'll be able to assess your Wild Weekend Units.

For your star meals you have the fun of making choices from those foods you like best. At a restaurant you may choose the avocado and prawn cocktail, the rack of lamb, or whatever you like. At a wedding you can toast the bride and groom in champagne and eat the wedding cake too. Even when you cook your favourite foods at home you'll be able to enjoy a delicious meal that suits your taste and your Wild Weekend budget.

Forthcoming attractions

To give you an idea of just how much fun The Wild Weekend Diet can be, let me tell you about a meal Irene, who lost 12 pounds (5.5 kg) on the plan, chose recently while dining out at an Italian restaurant.

She started her evening off with a glass of chianti. Red wine is her favourite choice no matter where or what she eats! She sipped her wine while munching the garlic bread, another favourite, and followed this with a first course of minestrone soup. By the time the main course came, she decided to have a second glass of wine, which she drank while eating veal parmigiana, spaghetti with tomato sauce, and sautéed courgettes with garlic. Irene chose tortoni for a sweet ending. All in all a very satisfying dinner.

Now let's see how the Italian dinner fitted into her Saturday night allotment of 22 Wild Weekend Units:

	WWUs
Chianti wine, 2 glasses	2
Minestrone soup, 1 mug	3
Garlic bread, 1 piece	2
Veal parmigiana	7
Spaghetti with tomato sauce, 1 mug	3
Sautéed courgettes	2
Tortoni	2
Coffee with cream	1
	22

Just think, the Italian dinner of her dreams added up to just 22 WWUs. It's a dieter's heaven!

The rest of the weekend

We've chosen Saturday night and Sunday lunch as the stars of your eating week. You follow a prescribed eating plan for the other weekend meals. Saturday breakfast, Saturday lunch, and Sunday breakfast and supper find you making limited choices and eating slim. The following list provides your weekend guide to success.

SATURDAY	SUNDAY
Breakfast	**Breakfast**
1 egg (poached or boiled) OR	2 oz (50 g) chicken or smoked haddock
2 oz (50 g) cottage cheese	½ mug orange or tomato juice
1 oz (25 g) wholemeal bread	1 oz (25 g) wholemeal bread
½ grapefruit or ½ mug orange juice	
Lunch	**Lunch**
3 oz (80 g) turkey or chicken OR	13 (15) WWUs
4 oz (115 g) cottage cheese	**Dinner**
1 oz (25 g) bread	3 oz (80 g) chicken or white fish salad with low calorie dressing
tomatoes, lettuce or green vegetables	small roll or 1 oz (25 g) bread
Dinner	
22 (29) WWUs	

Questions and answers

Question: I have only 5 pounds (2.25 kg) to lose. Will this diet work for me?
Answer: Yes. No matter how little or how much weight you want to lose, The Wild Weekend Diet will show you how to do it and how to maintain your new figure.

Question: May I change the weekend meal plan around and use my Wild Weekend Units on Friday night instead of Saturday night?
Answer: Yes. You may use your WWUs on any night of the weekend. In this case switch the whole day. On Friday, follow the Saturday meal plan for breakfast, lunch, and dinner. On Saturday follow the Weekday Slimdown Plan.

Question: Is this diet safe for everyone?
Answer: The Wild Weekend Diet is healthy and nutritious. If, however, you have a medical condition, follow the directions of your doctor; his or her advice always takes precedence. Special

advice for children and pregnant women can be found on pages 177 and 178.

Question: Do I have to eat breakfast? I'm just not hungry in the morning.
Answer: You'll want to keep your energy level on an even keel for when you need it the most. For that reason we recommend that you eat a separate meal in the morning and one in the afternoon.

Question: This diet seems to go against everything I have ever read about losing weight. How can I lose weight if I eat fish and chips and ice cream?
Answer: Food is neither bad nor good. All food contains calories. As long as the total number of calories you eat weekly is less than the number your body needs to maintain your current weight, you will lose weight. You can eat those calories in whatever weekend foods you choose.

Question: Do I have to use all my Wild Weekend Units?
Answer: No. You can save calories and lose weight faster by not using them all.

Question: I'm a junk-food junkie. My dream is to give up dinner on Saturday night and spend an entire evening eating junk foods. Will I lose weight if I do this?
Answer: Yes. As long as the foods you eat are within your total WWUs, eat away and have fun.

Question: I go home to my parents' every weekend. How will I know how to count Wild Weekend Units?
Answer: As you become familiar with the various foods on the lists in Chapters 7, 8 and 9, you will be able to make better and better judgments as to the number of WWUs that are contained in any particular food. When in doubt, count *high*.

Question: Is exercise necessary to lose weight on The Wild Weekend Diet?
Answer: The more you move, the more you'll lose, and faster too. The more you lose, the better you'll feel. Exercise is also recommended for overall good health. However, it is not a requirement for weight loss.

· CHAPTER THREE ·

OFF FOR THE WEEKEND

So now the diet begins. As you embark on the exciting Wild Weekend way to slimness you know a lot about this journey already. You know you can eat any food in the world, and you know you're going to be able to diet and satisfy your taste for your favourite foods. You know you can go to your favourite restaurant and no longer feel guilty when you order. You know that you can – and should – take the weekend off from a rigid diet plan.

Planning your spree

You have probably spent your whole week thinking about the foods you have been denied, but now you can choose what goodies to enjoy. Planning your spree is, of course, all-important. We suggest Saturday evening and Sunday lunch for your Wild Weekend meals, but if you prefer Friday and Saturday nights then the choice is yours – simply swap the three Friday meals for your Sunday meals and arrange them in the order you want, then return to your Weekday Slimdown Plan on Sunday.

Deciding how to spend your units is vital. Your budget is not unlimited but it is generous, and while we suggest a very high allocation of units on Saturday and fewer on Sunday – and our suggested menus are based on these figures – the choice is yours. You can 'buy' a dish for 3 WWUs or you can 'buy' one for 8. *You* decide how to use your WWUs for maximum satisfaction and enjoyment.

	SATURDAY	SUNDAY	TOTAL
Women	22	13	35
Men	29	15	44

Vive La Choice

You've worked for it, you've earned it, you deserve it and now it's yours. To help you make the most of your Wild Weekend here are some guidelines on how you can exercise your freedom of choice.

It is up to you to decide how you spend your Units. Is it a luscious chocolate profiterole dessert you long for as your grand finale, and the rest of the meal is inconsequential by comparison? Or do you crave a stiff gin and tonic (3 WWUs) and good bottle of wine (1 WWU per 4 fl oz [115 ml] glass) as a highlight to your evening? Or is it to be roast beef and Yorkshire pudding followed by steamed syrup sponge and custard? Whatever your preference, you need to know how many Wild Weekend Units your favourite foods and drinks will use up. Armed with this information you will be able to stay within your budget of Wild Weekend Units and remain confident that you can still lose weight.

So eat what you like. A long as you stay within your WWU budget you're doing fine.

Assessing your choice

Most people opt to spend most of their available WWUs on the main course. Three factors go into working out the WWUs of these and other dishes:

1. Choice

2. Portion size

3. Method of preparation

These are the components that determine the amount of WWUs any dish provides.

Choice

The main ingredient in any part of the meal will have a major effect on the WWUs. The higher the fat content of the ingredient, the higher its calorie content – or WWUs – will be. If we consider the main course, protein normally forms the basic part of the meal. The WWUs of fish, chicken, beef, pork and lamb vary according to the fat present within the different cuts of meat.

The following chart shows how much variation there will be in a cooked 6 oz (170 g) portion:

White fish (e.g. cod)	3 WWUs
Oily fish (e.g. salmon)	4 WWUs
Skinned chicken breast	4 WWUs
Top side roast beef (lean)	4 WWUs
Duck	7 WWUs
Marbled rib of roast beef	10 WWUs

Further lists will be found in Chapters 7–9 to help you in this choice.

Portion size

How much we eat or drink will considerably affect the number of WWUs in any meal, whether it is one glass of wine or three, a large or small portion. In this book we have presumed that a 6 oz (170 g) portion of cooked meat or fish would be a likely serving of these for Saturday dinner or Sunday lunch. It is important, therefore, that you learn to judge what a 6 oz (170 g) portion of cooked sausages, chicken, roast beef, steak, pork or lamb chop and beefburger looks like.

The illustrations will act as a guide, as will experience at home with the weighing scales. If your serving, when you eat your meal, is larger or smaller you should add or subtract WWUs accordingly.

Preparation

How food is cooked makes a large difference to its WWUs. It is no secret that grilled foods are lower in calories than fried and

THE WILD WEEKEND DIET

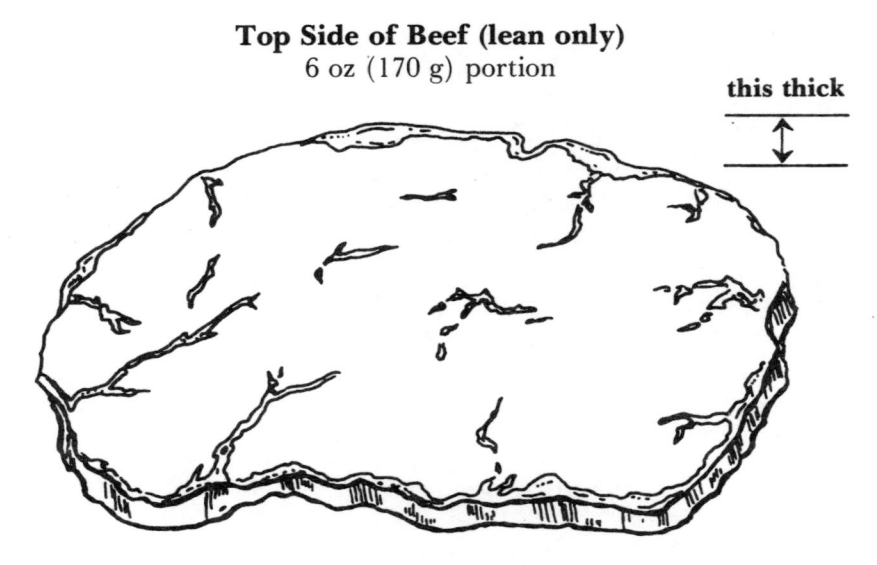

Top Side of Beef (lean only)
6 oz (170 g) portion

this thick

Two slices this size: 4 Units

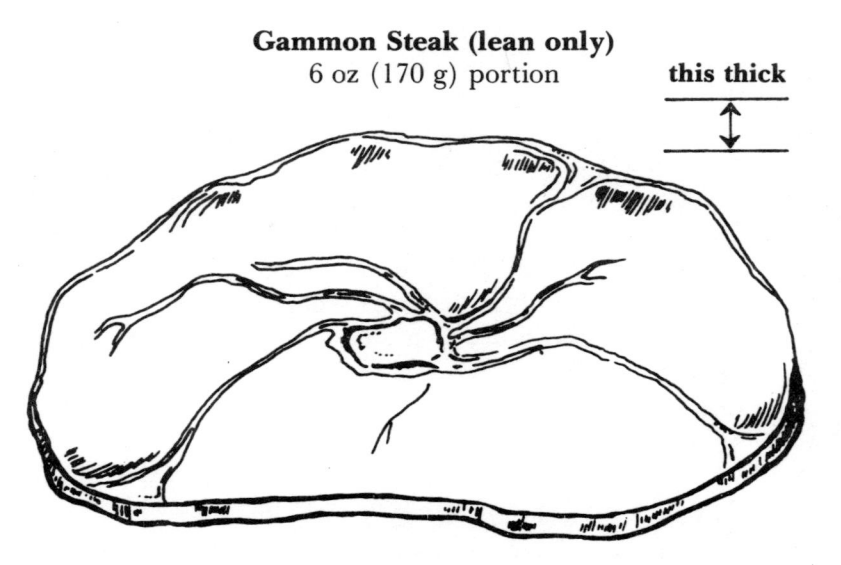

Gammon Steak (lean only)
6 oz (170 g) portion

this thick

Two slices this size: 3 Units

Lamb Chop (lean only)
6 oz (170 g) portion

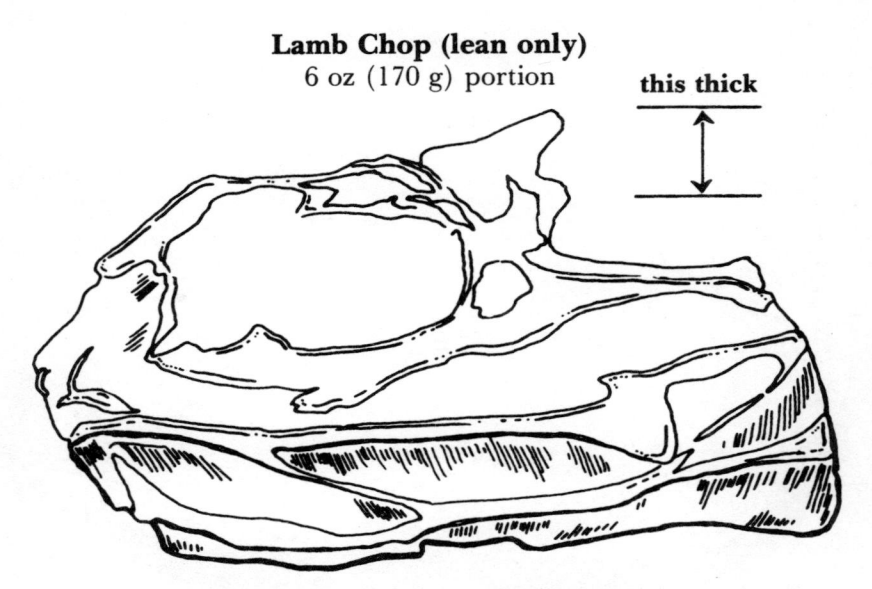

this thick

**One chop this size (fat removed): 3 Units
On the bone**

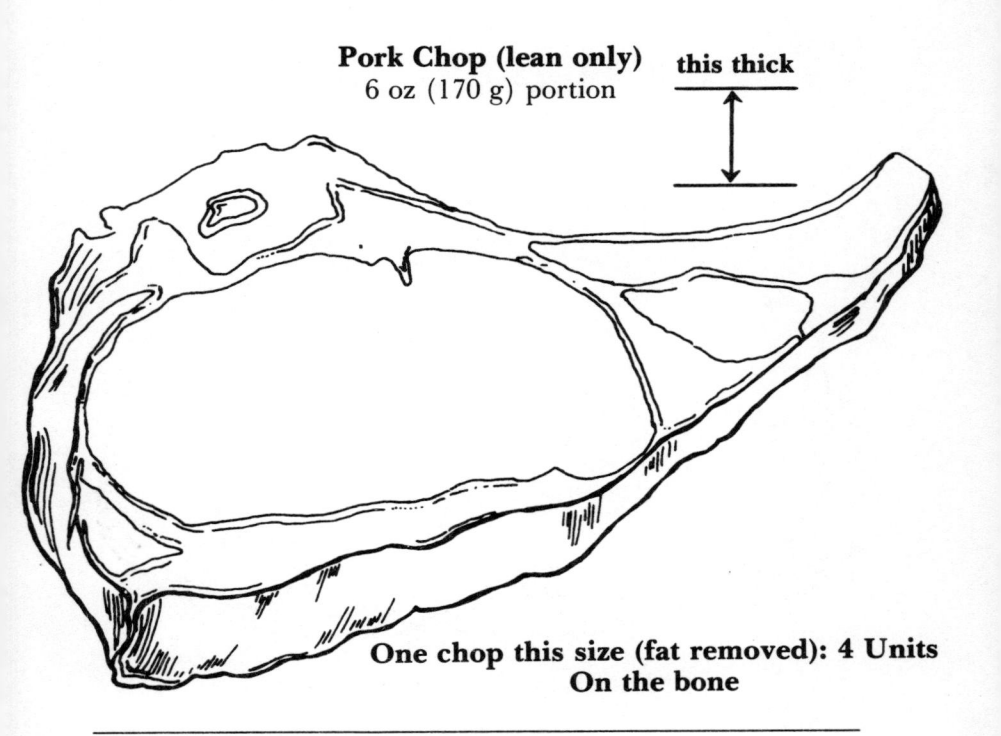

Pork Chop (lean only)
6 oz (170 g) portion

this thick

**One chop this size (fat removed): 4 Units
On the bone**

THE WILD WEEKEND DIET

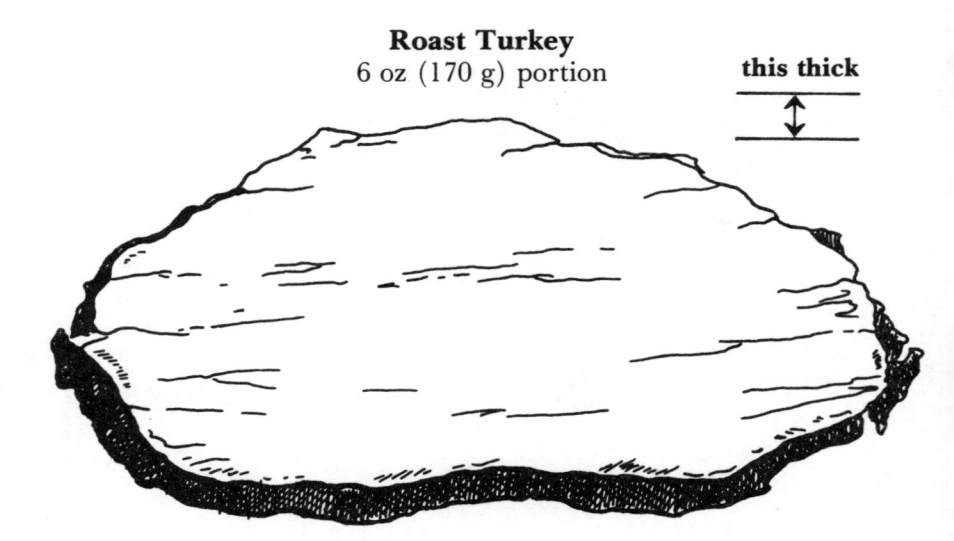

Roast Turkey
6 oz (170 g) portion

this thick

Two slices of light or dark meat this size: 4 Units

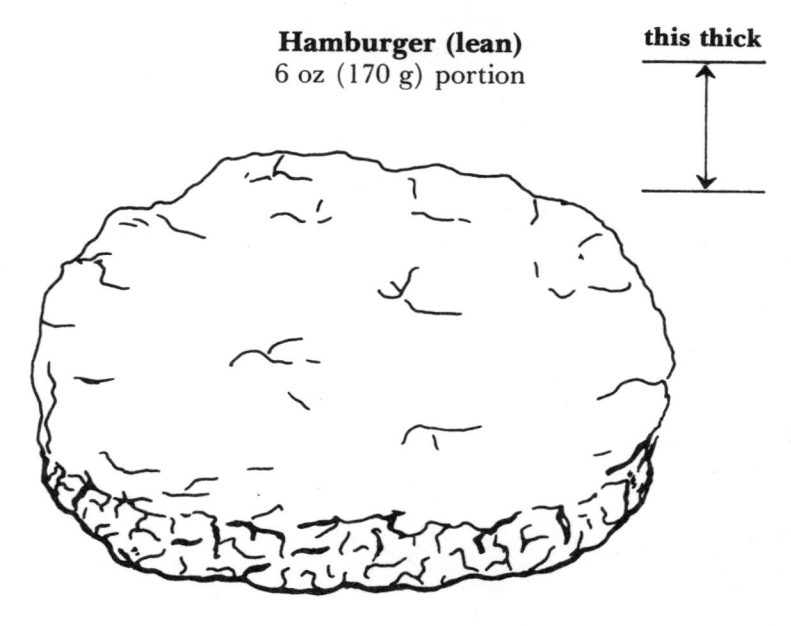

Hamburger (lean)
6 oz (170 g) portion

this thick

One burger this size: 4 Units

Rump Steak (lean only)
6 oz (170 g) portion

this thick

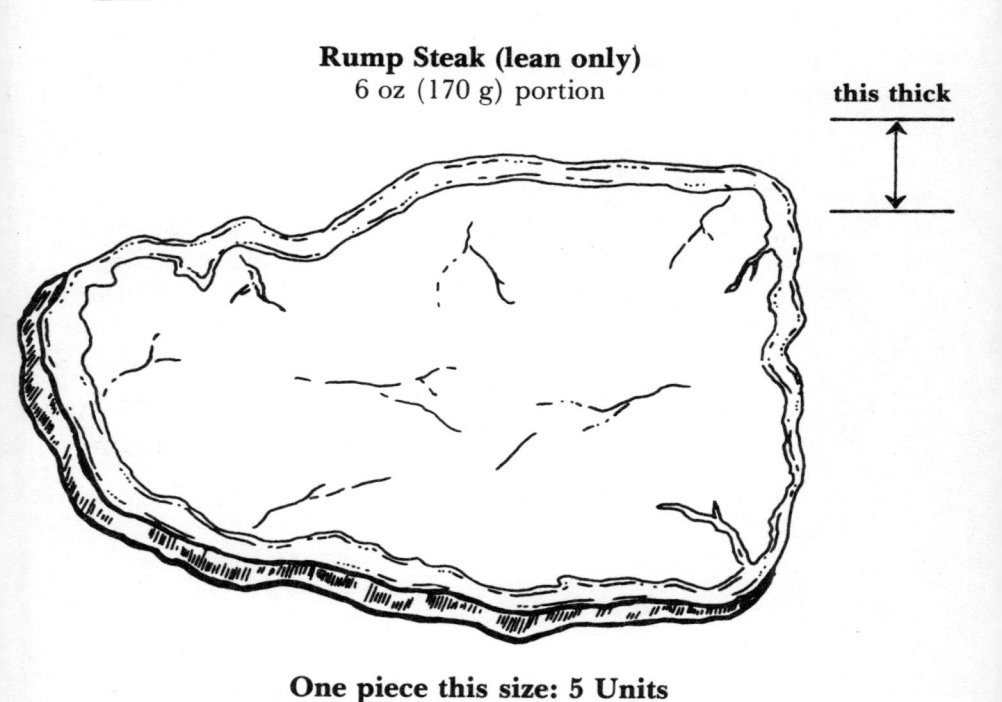

One piece this size: 5 Units

Veal (Escalope)
6 oz (170 g) portion

this thick

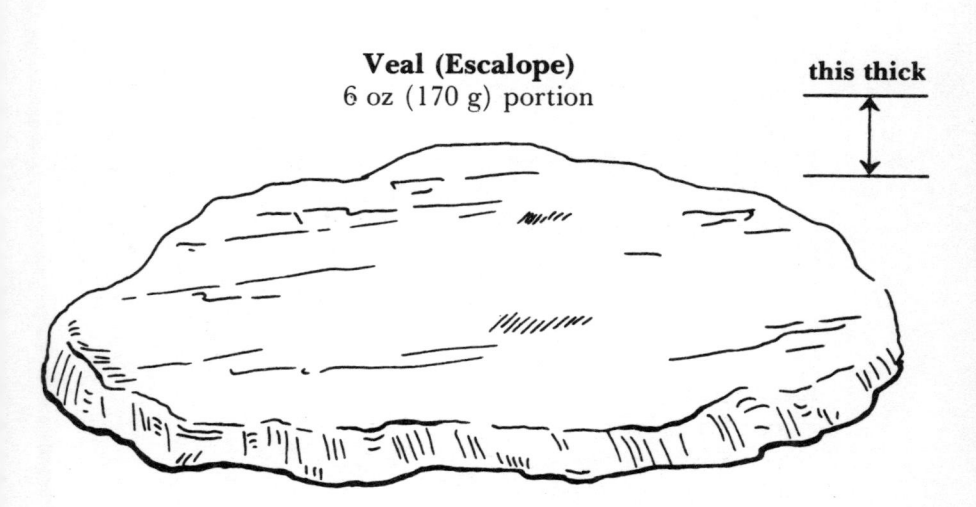

Two escalopes this size: 4 Units

that foods coated in batter or crumbs cost more in calories than their naked cousins.

To alert you to the expense of certain methods of food preparation, we are providing you with a Hot List. The Hot List is a complete guide to how methods of food preparation affect the total WWUs. Consider the following Hot List as you spend your WWU budget. Each of the following cooking methods costs you WWUs, which must be *added* to the total WWUs of any dish. Many dieters find this list too hot to handle!

Remember, your dish may have more than one Hot List item to be counted. Chicken may be coated *and* served with a sauce. Prawns can be fried *and* served in butter.

HOT LIST

COOKING METHOD	ADDITIONAL WWUs (*per 6 oz/170 g cooked protein, meat, fish, poultry*)
Au gratin	4 (minimum)
Barbecued	2
Basted	2
Béarnaise sauce	4
Braised	2
Breaded	2
Butter sauce	5
Buttery, buttered, served in butter	3
Cheesy, served with cheese	2
Cooked in oil, made with oil	3
Creamed	4 (minimum)
Cream sauce	4
Crispy	3
Escalloped	4 (minimum)
Fried	3
Fried in batter	5
Fried, served with tartar sauce	5

COOKING METHOD	ADDITIONAL WWUs *(per 6 oz/170 g cooked protein, meat, fish, poultry)*
Gravy, ½ mug homemade	4
Hollandaise sauce	5
In a tomato base	2
In pastry (fruit, dessert, etc.)	3
Sautéed	3
Sour cream	2
Stewed	1 (minimum)
Stir-fry (no fat added)	1
Stuffed	4
Sweet sauce	3
White sauce	3

If there is anything you don't understand on the menu, add 2 WWUs minimum just in case.

Now that we have 'heated' you up with the Hot List, we'll stop a minute and 'cool' you down with the Cool List. These are a dieter's best friend. None of these methods adds any extra WWUs to the base WWUs of the food item. Consider choosing these methods as you spend your Wild Weekend Units.

COOL LIST

Au bleu (poached trout)	Grilled
Baked	In its own juices (au jus)
Charcoal-grilled	Poached
Foil wrapped or in parchment paper (en papillotte)	Roasted on a rack
	Steamed
Garden fresh	With herbs (aux fines herbs)

Adding up

So, how does all this work?

Let's start by looking at the many variations of cooking

chicken and see how those cooking methods affect the WWUs. A serving of chicken (6 oz [170 g] cooked, skinless, white meat) has a base WWU of 4. If you choose a preparation from the Cool List, you keep your WWUs to an economical 4. That means, if you eat it grilled, baked, poached or steamed, or even charcoal-grilled, the WWUs remain at 4.

Let's say, though, that you're going to be adventurous and fry that chicken. This is a Hot List method of preparation, and it increases your WWU count by 3, for a total of 7 WWUs for the same 6 oz (170 g) of chicken. Perhaps you elect to complete your eating adventure with some cream sauce over the chicken. Add another 4 WWUs for a total of 11 WWUs — for the same amount of chicken.

Consider chicken cordon bleu. To tot up your WWUs you start again with the 4 of the plain, cooked chicken; add 2 WWUs for cheese; another 2 for ham; another 2 for breading; 3 for frying or baking in oil. And, of course, if you've topped it with a sauce or butter, add 3 WWUs for every 2 tablespoons. If you've followed all this addition, you'll find yourself counting the chicken cordon bleu as 16 WWUs. Here it is shown another way:

	WWUs
6 oz (170 g) chicken breast	4
1½ oz (40 g) cheese	2
1½ oz (40 g) ham	2
breading*	2
frying*	3
butter sauce*	3
	16

* All Hot List preparations are based on 6 oz (170 g) cooked protein.

What this tells you is that your adventure in eating an elaborately prepared main course such as chicken cordon bleu will cost you 16 Wild and Wonderful Weekend Units.

You can never go wrong if you count on the high side.

When you choose a portion size the exact number of WWUs of which you don't know, add additional WWUs to preserve your weight-loss goals.

Let me give you a few more examples on how to work out what various preparations 'cost' in terms of units.

If you want a large steak, 12 oz (350 g) of cooked beef, this means you have to double the basic 8 WWUs assigned for a 6 oz (170 g) portion. This makes 16 WWUs.

If you eat it charcoal-grilled, you begin and end with the 16 WWUs for 12 oz (350 g). But if you fry it, add 6 WWUs for the butter it is cooked in. Where did those 6 WWUs come from? Check the Hot List and you'll see frying 'costs' 3 WWUs for each 6 oz (170 g) of cooked protein. Since you doubled the portion, you must also double the WWU preparation cost.

You probably would not want more than 6 oz (170 g) of cooked beef casserole so here you start counting with the base cost of 8 WWUs and add 4 for the gravy, for a total of 13 WWUs.

12 oz (350 g) steak, grilled
   8 WWUs × 2   = 16 WWUs

12 oz (350 g) steak, fried
   8 WWUs × 2 + 3 WWUs × 2   = 22 WWUs

6 oz (170 g) beef casserole
   8 WWUs + 4 WWUs   = 12 WWUs

Fish is a dieter's best friend. It is the lowest in calories of all proteins and, ounce for ounce, offers high food value for very little WWU cost; i.e. poached salmon with herbs or grilled trout.

However, fish, just like chicken and beef, can be rendered high in WWUs by certain cooking methods. Let's take 6 oz (170 g) of haddock or any white-type fish. The base WWU for 6 oz (170 g) of haddock is 3. You can eat it grilled, baked, poached or steamed, and its WWU remains at 3.

Fish cooked in the above manner can be delicious, especially if not overcooked. But what if you love fried fish? Then you should choose a Hot List method and increase the WWUs by 3 for a total of 6 for the same piece of fish. And if tartar sauce is a favourite part of your fried fish, add another 3 WWUs for a total of 9.

Fish can be prepared in an infinite variety of ways. For the gourmet dish Sole Véronique, start with the base of 3 WWUs. Add 3 for the sauté preparation and then add 5 units for the butter sauce it swims in and an additional WWU for the white grapes in the sauce. You now have a total of 12 WWUs for Sole Véronique.

Let's look at Sole Véronique in more detail:

	WWUs
6 oz (170 g) sole	3
sautéed in butter	3*
butter sauce	5*
grapes	1
	12

* Hot List preparation 'cost' for 6 oz (170 g) of protein.

Baked and stuffed

When you sit down to eat fish, you may innocently assume that you are sitting down to a low-calorie dish. That is not necessarily true. Many a cordon bleu cook can pour on the cream and toss in the butter to make delicious dishes, but at what cost to dieters?

Wherever you see 'stuffed', think carefully. It is unlikely to be stuffed merely with a few spinach leaves or cottage cheese, even if these are claimed to be the contents. You can be pretty sure it will be packed with breadcrumbs and quantities of well disguised butter or cream which will toss on those extra WWUs and you will need to add a minimum of an extra 4 WWUs for EACH piece of food on your plate whether it's fillets of fish, joints of chicken, cutlets or chops of lamb or pork.

Remember, for dieters ignorance is not bliss. What may be a moment in the mouth can be a lifetime on the hips.

Points to consider

Enjoy making your food choices on The Wild Weekend Diet! This is a unique approach to weight loss, and you will be successful as long as you take some time with it. *But you are not relieved of taking responsibility for the foods you eat.* Although you will find WWUs for many foods in this book, they are only reliable estimates based on standard, accepted recipes; variations in foods and food preparation do occur. You have all the choices, but use your head. As you eat a food, bring into action all of your senses (sight, smell, touch, sound and taste) to help you more accurately to assess the WWUs of a food. Ask yourself these questions:

- Is there more here than the standard WWU portion size?
- Does this food taste especially oily, buttery or greasy?
- Does this food taste unusually sweet?
- Does this food feel greasy in my mouth? (This is particularly important if you've ordered a food prepared without oil or butter.)
- Is the word *smothered* used in describing the food?
- Does this food smell or taste differently than it should? Is there a hint of frying or sautéing?
- Is this food garnished with items not included in my total WWUs?
- Is there a greasy residue left on the plate?
- Is there heavy marbling of fat in a beef or ham serving?

For every yes answer to the above questions add at least 2 WWUs to the WWU total of that dish.

You'll never go wrong if you count too high. You'll only lose weight a little faster!

It's Saturday night

Whether you're home or abroad, in a restaurant, visiting

friends or attending a special event, your time of decision has arrived. It is Saturday night on your Wild Weekend Diet. The only thing that stands between you and what you eat is your decision. Let's try out the system, remembering how many units you have to spend.

> **SATURDAY WWUS**
>
> 22 WWUs for women
> 29 WWUs for men

Logically we begin at the beginning. Even moderate drinkers find Saturday night a time to enjoy one or two drinks and some wine. Cocktails range from 2–4 WWUs per glass, so if you choose 2 gin and tonics before your meal this will be 4 WWUs (only 3 if you ask for Slimline tonic). Peanuts will use up a hefty 5 WWUs for 2 oz (50 g) so make sure you do not absent-mindedly sit by a plate of these unless you *plan* to eat them.

Soups or other starters will be the first part of your meal. They may range from a low 1 WWU to a high 7 WWUs. Bear this in mind as you think ahead of the meal to come. If you are at a restaurant, cooking for a supper party or having a simple meal at home, remember the choice is yours. If you decide on a prawn cocktail that will be 2 WWUs, making a total of 6 WWUs so far. If, on the other hand, you are dining out at family or friends' you will seem churlish to turn down the starter, but you can say no to garlic bread, croûtons or a roll and butter – a wise precaution if you think there are many tempting items to follow.

Your main course can be considered in three separate sections: the main dish (meat, fish, etc.), the starch (potatoes, pasta, rice or bread) and the vegetables. Many of the latter are, of course, free. If you were to have the following meal and with it two glasses of wine, you would have used up 18 WWUs as follows:

		WWUs
Drinks	2 Gin and tonic	4
	2 glasses white wine	2
Starter	Prawn cocktail	2
Main dish	Steak and kidney pie (6 oz [170 g] portion)	7
Starch	Medium baked potato with ½ oz (12 g) butter	3
Vegetables	Green beans (no butter)	0
		18

Only when you have worked out your total so far can you decide how to finish your meal. You must assess whether you can afford to have dessert, or just fruit, biscuits and cheese, coffee with cream, liqueur or brandy.

If you are a woman you still have 4 WWUs in hand. A man will have 11 more WWUs to spend. Your black coffee and tea are WWU free, but if you add sugar, milk or cream add 1 WWU for each. The choice for a woman is likely to be limited to dessert or cheese, whereas a man could probably afford to eat both, as you will see from the following example.

		WWUs
Dessert	Lemon soufflé	3
Cheese	Biscuits and cheese (no butter)	3
Beverage	Coffee with cream	1
After dinner	Brandy	1
		8

A wonderful meal if you are a man – you can afford a second helping of pudding. And if you are a woman you can skip the cheese and the cream or brandy and stay right on course for losing weight.

Sunday lunches

For many, habits die hard. A drink beforehand, followed by a traditional Sunday roast, is what we all love. So how can this be accommodated on our allocation of WWUs for Sunday lunch? If you have spent your Saturday allocation you have:

> SUNDAY WWUs
>
> 13 WWUs for women
> 15 WWUs for men

to complete your Wild Weekend.

A typical Sunday mid-day meal might be:

		WWUs
Pre-lunch drink	Can of beer or large sherry	2
Meat	2 slices roast sirloin or topside (4 oz [115 g] lean, no fat)	3
	Gravy, ½ mug tinned	2
	1 teaspoon horseradish sauce (not cream)	0
	Mustard	0
Starch	2 small roast potatoes	2
	small Yorkshire pudding	2
Vegetables	Brussels sprouts	0
	Carrots	0
Dessert	Apple pie (no cream)	4
Beverage	Black coffee	0
		15

A man may enjoy his Sunday favourites and still keep within his budget. A woman will have to make some savings as she has only 13 WWUs to spend. Foregoing a pre-lunch drink or potatoes would be one solution, or replace the apple pie with a piece of fresh fruit if you prefer. Remember you can always *save* units from Saturday night, so long as you don't exceed the weekend total you are still on target for slimming success.

Next weekend

This weekend we planned together. Next week you're on your own. By the time you finish this book you will know how you want to spend your Wild Weekend Units. You will know everything you need to know before you enjoy your meal because you will find all the WWU information in Chapters 7, 8 and 9. Spend some time now to browse through these chapters, as you would a mail-order catalogue. By the time you are ready to spend WWUs you will have a good idea of how to fit the foods you love into your WWU budget. Have fun, and *bon appétit!*

· CHAPTER FOUR ·

WEEKDAY SLIMDOWN PLAN

Smile!

The Wild Weekend is coming!

At first glance the Weekday Slimdown Plan (WSP) looks much like other low-calorie diets, but it isn't. The difference lies in the role that the WSP plays in The Wild Weekend Diet as a whole.

The WSP is the heart of The Wild Weekend Diet. It is a no-choice, carefully planned and satisfying diet. Its structure provides the support you need for weight-loss success. It is a 5-day discipline with the promise of change ahead. We are all used to 5-day commitment – and need our weekend break!

The operative word here is *control*. Controlled eating equals controlled calories, and controlled calories equal weight loss and weight control.

Monday to Friday, you set your alarm clock. When it rings, you don't think about it, you get up. It's the same with the WSP. Don't think about it during the week, just do it! Because when the weekend comes, you've got a lovely morning's sleep to look forward to, and even lovelier WWUs to spend.

Creating our overdraft

The Weekday Slimdown Plan provides 4,000 calories a week for women and 5,200 calories for men. All of these calories are consumed from Monday to Friday. During this time women will be eating only about 800 calories per day and men will be eating 1,040 which is far less energy than your body needs to operate. This is the time, therefore, when your body will be burning up the energy you've stored away as fat.

If you and The Wild Weekend Diet are to work together as a successful partnership, you must adhere strictly to guidelines. You cannot allow yourself any additions or exchanges that might in some way interfere with your weight loss. Adding extra food or beverages to the WSP will slow your weight loss down considerably.

Enjoy your controlled routine in the same way you enjoy a more structured lifestyle during the week. And all the while you are following the WSP, enjoy thinking that this is the time you are burning up those unwanted pounds and inches.

Temptations

Well-meaning friends, television commercials, newspaper and magazine advertisements, supermarket strategy, co-workers, family, etc., will each, at some time, give you permission to go off the diet and will always create detours and roadblocks on your road to success. Depend on it. You are going to face temptations every step of the way. That's life. But, forewarned is forearmed. Stand up to these temptations and remind yourself that the weekend is coming.

Be wise; be one step ahead. The best defence against being undermined is your own resolve. Put yourself in charge of your eating and your weight loss. Taking care of your responsibilities is your best protection against miseating.

Another kind of temptation is the one that beckons you to skip a meal here or a part of a meal there. This habit will erode the most fervent goals. It is well known that breakfast skippers experience a strong late-afternoon food urge, as well as an energy lag. And that's only part of the problem that comes from meal skipping. More insidious is that feeling of entitlement the skipper gets which allows her/him to feel he deserves that 'little something' in exchange for the foods she/he's given up. That 'little something' rarely takes the form of a crispbread or raw carrot.

WSP strategy

As with any plan of action, any worthy objective, there must be a strategy. Your objective is losing those pounds and inches. This is your goal. With the goal firmly in sight, strategy defines the method used to reach the goal. The strategy for the WSP is *getting ready*, by psyching yourself up, *getting set*, by arranging your life so that you can diet well, and *go*, with the plans we provide.

Getting ready

The best time to begin this step is, of course, right now. From this minute on, think of yourself as ready to start your most exciting diet, a diet that is so well fashioned it meets your every need. What a truly clever person you are to have discovered it!

Keep getting ready by telling yourself each day that you will succeed on The Wild Weekend Diet. Why wouldn't you? Tell yourself that it is your ultimate and your last diet. Convince yourself deep down inside that you are a winner and that you can do the things you want to do. And what you want to do now is to get thin!

Close your eyes and picture yourself as a thin person ... more attractive, more self-confident, healthier, doing the things you want to do, looking the way you want to look, having more energy. Bring this picture back to your mind every single day as soon as you wake up, and again just before you go to sleep, and at any time during the day when you may doubt your ability to succeed. If you can dream it and keep that dream in front of you, you will succeed.

Think of losing weight as your right. You, too, have the right to be healthier. And to have a more exciting lifestyle. Keep telling yourself this. This is your last diet. Believe it.

Getting set

There are two parts to getting started: one is getting rid of the things you don't want in the house; the second is to get the food and equipment you need to follow the WSP.

Each of us finds certain foods and/or situations hard to handle when we're dieting.

Some people succumb to the smell of freshly baked biscuits. Others have trouble getting the mixture into the oven. Still others find food a comfort when anxiety is high, or as a friend when no one else is around. Some people let themselves get so hungry that they eat before they even sit down at the table. For some of us, eating with friends gives us permission to eat as they eat. Only you know what your pitfalls are. Think ahead to those foods and situations that have to be handled now. Don't think about what your family needs to eat, think in terms of what you can't handle around the house. Don't promise yourself to be strong. You don't need to be a tower of strength, you just need to be successful at weight loss.

As far as hard-to-handle situations are concerned, think about what you can do to improve or avoid them. By all means ask for the help of those involved. Together you can brainstorm new ideas on controlling those difficulties we all have. Plan now. Failing to plan is planning to fail. You owe it to yourself to put some time in on this project.

Go shopping and spend what you must to have the foods and tools at hand that will get you through. Use these two lists as your guidelines to success.

WEIGHT CONTROL TOOLS

- Diet or postage scales – accurate to at least ¼ oz (7 g): Will weigh meats, fish, poultry, cheese, fruit and vegetables, cereals and bread. Kitchen scales give too much scope for cheating, but diet scales are precise and available from chainstores and large chemists (order if not in stock).
- Measuring jug: To measure milk, juices and other drinks.
- Measuring spoons: To measure diet salad dressings and diet jam.
- 8 fl oz (225 ml) mug: To measure vegetables, liquids, etc.
- Non-stick pan: So food can be dry fried, etc., without fat.
- Food diary: To use daily to plan your menu or to keep a record of anything that passes your lips. This is an excellent habit to acquire.

- Shopping list: To use weekly to be sure you always have the WSP foods you need to hand – and to avoid impulse buying and impulse eating.

SHOPPING LIST FOR WSP PLAN

Artificial sweeteners
   (low sodium recommended)

Bean sprouts

Beef extract (Bovril)

Bouillon cubes

Breads
   Muffins, wholemeal
   Pumpernickel
   Rye
   Wholemeal bread
   Wholemeal rolls
   Wholewheat pitta

Cereals unsweetened
   All Bran
   Bran Flakes
   Oat flakes
   Oatmeal
   Puffed Wheat
   Shredded Wheat
   Unsweetened muesli
   Wheat flakes

Cheese
   Low fat Cheddar
   Low fat cottage
   Parmesan

Coffee

Consommé

Eggs (No. 3 or 4)

Essence
   Vanilla
   Brandy, etc.

Fish, white or shellfish
   Cod
   Coley
   Crab
   Haddock (fresh or smoked)
   Halibut
   Mussels
   Prawns

Fish, oily
   Kippers (frozen without butter)
   Trout
   Tuna – tinned, brine packed

Fruit, fresh
   Apples
   Apricots
   Blackberries
   Cantaloupe melon
   Currants
   Gooseberries
   Nectarines
   Oranges

Peaches
Pineapple
Plums

Fruit, tinned in unsweetened
    fruit juice
  Apricots
  Dietetic fruits
  Mandarins
  Peaches
  Pineapple

Fruit juices, unsweetened
    natural juices
  Apple
  Citrus juices
  Pineapple
  Tomato

Herbs and spices
  All fresh and dried herbs
    and spices
  Garlic
  Horseradish sauce
  Mustard
  Onion flakes
  Pepper
  Salt

Jams
  Diet fruit jam
  Diet marmalade

Leafy greens
  Brussels sprouts
  Cabbage (red, white and
    green)
  Chicory
  Chinese leaves
  Cress

  Lettuce
  Spinach
  Spring greens
  Watercress

Meat
  Chicken breast (skinned)
  Liver of any kind
  Turkey breast
  Veal

Milk
  Skimmed Long Life
  Skimmed non-fat dried
  Skimmed pasteurised

Pop, diet/one-cal. fizzy
    drinks

Salad dressing diet/low cal.

Sauces
  Soy
  Tabasco
  Worcestershire

Spa waters, Perrier, Vichy,
    etc.

Sugar free soda water

Tea

Tofu

Vegetables (fresh, frozen,
    tinned) of your choice
  Asparagus
  Aubergines
  Carrots
  Cauliflower
  Celery
  Courgettes

Fennel	Sweetcorn
Green beans	Tomatoes
Mange-tout	
Mushrooms	Vinegar
Onions	
Peas	Yeast extract
Peppers	Yogurt, plain low fat

Now get a piece of paper and make a shopping list. Go through your cupboards and refrigerator and write down what you need. Clear the shelves of all temptations. You must have all the right foods in your home ahead of time so you will not be faced with the dilemma of what to eat. The WSP menus let you know exactly what you will be eating.

Go!

It's time to begin. Start today on the Weekday Slimdown Plan. And, just this once, *diet through the first weekend following the Weekday Slimdown Plan with no Wild Weekend*. This is very important.

- You put yourself in a diet frame of mind.
- You remove yourself from anytime, anywhere, and any-old-thing eating.

Here are the WSP guidelines you will follow. Perhaps they sound familiar? That is because it is well known that they are essential for people who want to get thin on a healthy diet.

1. Bake, boil, steam, grill, charcoal grill or poach all meats, fish and poultry.
2. Remove all visible fat before cooking.
3. Remove all poultry and fish skin before eating. Before cooking is preferable.
4. Use no added fats or oils in cooking or food preparations; e.g., mayonnaise, butter, etc.
5. Weigh all meats, fish, poultry, *after* cooking to be sure you are eating the correct amount.**
6. Weigh all breads and hard cheese.

7. Measure the fruits and vegetables and cottage cheese as required.
8. Use a non-stick pan to fry or scramble your eggs.

WEEKLY MEAL PATTERN

Sunday	Monday	Tuesday	Wednesday	Thursday	Friday	Saturday
Slimdown Breakfast						Saturday Breakfast
Wild Weekend Lunch 13 (15) WWUs	Weekday Slimdown Plan WSP	Weekday Slimdown Plan WSP	Weekday Slimdown Plan WSP	Weekday Slimdown Plan WSP	Weekday Slimdown Plan WSP	Saturday Lunch
Sunday Supper						Wild Weekend Dinner 22 (29) WWUs

**Note: 1 lb (450 g) of raw meat, fish or skinless, boneless chicken yields 12 oz (350 g) cooked meat; 8 oz (225 g) raw equals 6 oz (170 g) cooked meat, fish, or poultry.

1 lb (450 g) of raw chicken with skin and bone yields 10 oz (280 g) cooked. 2½ lb (1.25 kg) bag frozen chicken breasts equals 4 portions.

WSP DAILY ALLOWANCES

DAY 1

Breakfast:
1 egg No. 3–4
1 oz (25 g) wholemeal bread
1 orange, small

Lunch:
5 oz (140 g) cottage cheese
1 oz (25 g) wholemeal bread
Fresh vegetables/salad

Dinner:
4 oz (115 g) white fish
½ mug peas
Free vegetables/salad

Snack:
8 fl oz (225 ml) skimmed milk
Permitted fruit

DAY 2

Breakfast:
2 oz (50 g) cottage cheese
¾ oz (20 g) unsweetened muesli
4 oz (115 g) pineapple chunks, packed in own juice

Lunch:
3 oz (80 g) turkey breast
1 oz (25 g) wholemeal bread
Fresh vegetables/salad

Dinner:
4 oz (115 g) liver
½ mug onions
Free vegetables/salad

Snack:
8 fl oz (225 ml) skimmed milk
Permitted fruit

DAY 3

Breakfast:
1 oz (25 g) Cheddar cheese
1 oz (25 g) wholemeal bread
½ pint (300 ml) tomato juice

Lunch:
3 oz (80 g) tuna, brine packed
2 thick rye crispbreads
Free vegetables/salad

Dinner:
4 oz (115 g) chicken
½ mug parsnip, leek or beetroot
Free vegetables/salad

Snack:
8 fl oz (225 ml) skimmed milk
Permitted fruit

DAY 4

Breakfast:
2 oz (50 g) cottage cheese
4 oz (115 g) cooked porridge
4 fl oz (115 ml) orange juice

Lunch:
3 oz (80 g) soft tofu OR
3 oz (80 g) frozen shellfish
1 oz (25 g) wholemeal bread
Free vegetables/salad

Dinner:
4 oz (115 g) veal or lean beef
½ mug sweetcorn/broad beans
Free vegetables/salad

Snack:
8 fl oz (225 ml) skimmed milk
Permitted fruit

WSP DAILY ALLOWANCES

DAY 5

Breakfast:
1 egg No. 3–4
1 oz (25 g) All bran
4 fl oz (115 ml) grapefruit juice

Lunch:
3 oz (80 g) chicken breast
1 oz (25 g) wholemeal bread
Free vegetables/salad

Dinner:
4 oz (115 g) turkey breast
½ mug potatoes or swede OR
4 oz (115 g) jacket potato
Free vegetables

Snack:
8 fl oz (225 ml) skimmed milk
Permitted fruit

N.B. Weights for meat, fish and poultry are cooked weights.

Free vegetables and salads: Cauliflower, broccoli, sprouts, cabbage and other leafy greens and salads, celery, French and runner beans, carrots, courgettes, cucumber, peppers and tomatoes.

Permitted fruit: 1 small apple, peach, nectarine, orange, pear, or large plum. 2 oz (50 g) berries or blackcurrants. 4 oz (115 g) wedge honeydew (cantaloupe) melon.

Free flavours: Artificial sweetener, coffee, diet drinks, diet salad dressing (1 tablespoon per day), diet jam (2 teaspoons per day), herbs, flavouring essence, lemon, lime, mustard, stock cubes, soy sauce, spices, tea, vinegar, water, Worcestershire sauce, yeast extract.

Men only: Add daily 2 oz (50 g) bread and 3 oz (80 g) cooked meat, fish or poultry.

- **Any whole day may be exchanged for any other whole day.**

Special diets for teenagers are on the next page or in the Core Diet (page 165). Diets for expectant and nursing mothers are on page 178.

TEENAGE ADDITIONS TO WSP AND WEEKEND MEALS

GIRLS

BOYS

MONDAY–FRIDAY

Follow WSP and add:
12 fl oz (350 ml) skimmed milk or very low fat yogurt
2 apples or oranges
1 oz (25 g) meat, fish or poultry

Follow WSP and add:
12 fl oz (350 ml) skimmed milk or very low fat yogurt
4 oz (115 g) of cooked meat, fish or poultry
1 oz (25 g) wholemeal bread
2 apples or oranges
8 fl oz (225 ml) tomato juice or ½ grapefruit

SATURDAY

Saturday breakfast:
1 egg or 2 oz (50 g) cottage cheese
1 oz (25 g) wholemeal bread
4 fl oz (115 ml) orange or grapefruit juice

Saturday lunch:
3 oz (80 g) cottage cheese, chicken or turkey breast
1 oz (25 g) wholemeal bread
Lettuce, tomatoes or other free vegetables
½ mug berries or ½ mug fruit packed in its own juice

Saturday night:
12 Wild Weekend Units

Saturday breakfast:
1 egg or 2 oz (50 g) cottage cheese
1 oz (25 g) wholemeal bread
4 fl oz (115 ml) orange or grapefruit juice

Saturday lunch:
3 oz (80 g) cottage cheese, chicken or turkey breast
1 oz (25 g) wholemeal bread
Lettuce, tomatoes or other free vegetables
½ mug berries or ½ mug fruit packed in its own juice

Saturday night:
12 Wild Weekend Units

WEEKDAY SLIMDOWN PLAN

GIRLS

Snacks or anytime:
12 fl oz (300 ml) skimmed milk or very low fat yogurt
2 apples or oranges
1 oz (25 g) meat, fish or poultry

BOYS

Snacks or anytime:
12 fl oz (300 ml) skimmed milk or very low fat yogurt
4 oz (115 g) cooked meat, fish, or poultry
1 oz (25 g) wholemeal bread
2 apples or oranges
8 fl oz (225 ml) tomato juice or ½ grapefruit

SUNDAY

Sunday breakfast:
1 egg or 2 oz (50 g) smoked haddock
1 oz (25 g) bread
4 fl oz (115 ml) orange juice

Sunday lunch:
9 Wild Weekend units

Sunday night:
4 oz (115 g) plain chicken, turkey or fish
3 oz (80 g) peas or sweetcorn
Free vegetables
½ mug fruit, unsweetened

Snacks or anytime:
10 fl oz (280 ml) skimmed milk or very low fat yogurt
2 oz (50 g) meat, fish or poultry
2 apples or oranges

Sunday breakfast:
1 egg or 2 oz (50 g) smoked haddock
1 oz (25 g) bread
4 fl oz (115 ml) orange juice

Sunday lunch:
9 Wild Weekend Units

Sunday night:
4 oz (115 g) plain chicken, turkey or fish
3 oz (80 g) peas or sweetcorn
Free vegetables
½ mug fruit, unsweetened

Snacks or anytime:
12 fl oz (300 ml) skimmed milk or very low fat yogurt
5 oz (140 g) cooked meat, fish or poultry
2 apples or oranges
8 fl oz (225 ml) tomato juice or ½ grapefruit

Eating on the WSP need not be bland and boring. You'll be amazed just what you can do to add zest and zip to low-calorie meals. We have taken out the calories, and now we'll show you how to add flavour and appeal.

Flavour tips

You may not be able to cook in butter on the WSP or spark up a sizzling flaming steak with brandy, but you can add the flavour to your meals by using rum, brandy, or sherry essence which are readily available.

The average UK citizen consumes a staggering 5 oz (140 g) sugar per day – give this up and you will automatically lose ½ lb (¼ kilo) per week. Add to this an intake of, say, 1 lb (½ kilo) of butter or margarine per week – only 2½ oz (65 g) per day is very easily consumed – and this will give 1 lb (½ kilo) of weight loss with ease. Substitutes for making food taste just as good are easily found.

Here are some flavourful suggestions:

- Use a non-stick pan to dry fry eggs, fish, and skinned chicken breasts.
- Sauté vegetables in one tablespoon of water with half to one bouillon cube or one tablespoon of aspic powder.
- Shake a small amount of grated Parmesan cheese on steamed vegetables or grilled fish.
- Marinate vegetables, fish, chicken or turkey in diet salad dressing for added succulence.
- Use flavoured vinegars and a variety of mustards for delicious salads.
- Become a spice-and-herb connoisseur and experiment with different combinations on vegetables and meats.
- Use lemon juice from a bottle or squeeze it on fresh. Wonderful on vegetables.
- Dab a little soy or teriyaki sauce on fish or chicken for an Oriental flair. Or try Tabasco or Worcestershire sauce to stimulate the senses.

De-lite-ful recipes for you

Be creative as you prepare your WSP meals. To get you started here are some delicious recipes for you to use. Each recipe follows the guidelines for the WSP. Milk or low fat yogurt should be subtracted from the daily milk allowance.

BREAKFAST RECIPES

Knights of Windsor
(Eggy Bread)

DAY 1

1 egg, size 3 or 4
2 tablespoons skimmed milk
Few drops vanilla essence

2 artificial sweeteners
1 large thin slice wholemeal bread
(1 oz/25 g)

Whisk together egg, milk, essence and sweeteners. Cut bread in half, place on a plate and pour the egg mixture over. Leave to soak. Heat medium-sized non-stick frying pan and wipe sparingly with kitchen paper dipped in oil. Lift bread into pan, top with any remaining mixture and cook until golden underneath before turning with a fish slice.
SERVES 1

VARIATION: Use very low fat yogurt instead of milk.
WSP NOTE: Milk from daily allowance.

Fruity Muesli

DAY 2

¼ mug unsweetened muesli
4 oz (115 g) pineapple chunks packed in own juice
2 oz (50 g) cottage cheese

2 tablespoons low fat yogurt
2 teaspoons diet marmalade
few drops liquid sweetener
(optional)

Soak muesli with pineapple and its juice overnight. In the morning toss with cottage cheese.
SERVES 1

VARIATION: Add very low fat yogurt and diet marmalade or sweetener from daily allowance.

Bubbling Cheese Breakfast   DAY 3

1 oz (25 g) grated Cheddar cheese
1 medium slice wholemeal bread
   (1 oz/25 g)

2 dashes Worcestershire sauce

Toast bread on one side. Turn over and top with cheese and splash with Worcestershire sauce. Grill till the cheese bubbles.

Cinnamon Toasts   DAY 4

2 oz (50 g) cottage cheese
Cinnamon to taste
Liquid artificial sweetener

2 small slices very thick wholemeal
   bread (1 oz/25 g)
(Bread used to replace porridge on
   chart)

Mix cottage cheese, cinnamon and sweetener together. Spread on toast and bake in oven at 350°F, 180°C, Gas mark 4, for 6–7 minutes.
SERVES 1

Sunny Tarragon Eggs   DAY 5

2 large or 4 × 1 oz (25 g) pitta
   breads
4 teaspoons French mustard

2 teaspoons tarragon
4 eggs No. 3–4
Salt and pepper to taste

Split pitta breads, spread with mustard and sprinkle with tarragon. Toast both sides. Set on non-stick baking tray and break two eggs on large or 1 egg on each small pitta bread. Slip under pre-heated grill about 6 inches (15 cm) from heat and cook 4–5 minutes until eggs are set. Garnish with parsley if wished.
SERVES 4

LUNCH RECIPES

Toasted Mackerel Sandwich DAY 1 (cold)

1½ oz (40 g) smoked mackerel
2 oz (50 g) cottage cheese
1 teaspoon horseradish
1 tablespoon Thousand Island diet dressing

Crisp lettuce
1 tomato
2 small slices thin brown bread, toasted (1 oz/25 g)

Mash together mackerel, cottage cheese, horseradish and dressing.
  Spread on toast and top with sliced tomato and lettuce.
SERVES 1

WSP NOTE: Portion of cottage cheese exchanged for portion of mackerel with similar calorie and food value.

Celery Chowder DAY 1 (hot)

3 sticks celery, sliced thinly
½ mug shredded white cabbage
½ green pepper
¼ teaspoon garlic salt
½ beef stock cube

8 fl oz (225 ml) boiling water
½ slice thick brown bread, diced (1 oz/25 g)
5 oz (140 g) cottage cheese
2 tablespoons chopped parsley

Simmer celery, cabbage and pepper in water with garlic salt and stock cube until tender, 10–15 minutes.
  Toast bread cubes until dry and crisp.
  Remove soup from heat, stir in cottage cheese and parsley. Reheat soup without boiling and serve immediately, scattered with the croûtons.
SERVES 1

Crunchy Turkey Salad   DAY 2 (cold)

3 oz (80 g) cooked turkey, diced
½ thick slice wholemeal bread, diced
(1 oz/25 g)
1 small head fennel, sliced
½ mug shredded white cabbage
1 tablespoon diet French dressing
Pepper
2 teaspoons lemon juice

Grill diced bread slowly until dry and crispy. Toss all ingredients together and serve immediately.
SERVES 1

VARIATION: Good with chicken or tuna.

Turkey Goulash   DAY 2 (hot)

3½ oz (100 g) raw turkey breast,
   cut in small fingers
2 teaspoons mild paprika
1 medium courgette, sliced
2 oz (50 g) button mushrooms
2 tomatoes, sliced
½ red pepper, sliced
1 artificial sweetener
¼ teaspoon garlic salt
Freshly ground black pepper
¾ oz (20 g) noodles, cooked

Place all ingredients, except noodles, in a covered non-stick pan with turkey at the bottom. Cover and cook gently for 15 minutes until turkey is cooked. Then uncover and cook briskly for 2–3 minutes if necessary to reduce juices in pan.

Serve with noodles and if wished sauerkraut and 1–2 tablespoons of yogurt.
SERVES 1

WSP NOTE: Noodles exchanged from bread allowance. Yogurt, if used, from daily milk quota.

Lebanese Tuna Salad   DAY 3 (cold)

½ chicken stock cube
4 fl oz (115 ml) boiling water
3 oz (80 g) tuna in brine
¾ oz (20 g) bulgar wheat
¼ cucumber, diced
2 spring onions, chopped
1 tablespoon diet French dressing
1 teaspoon lemon juice
1 teaspoon chopped mint
½ bunch watercress

Mix stock cube with boiling water and juices from tuna. Add bulgar wheat and leave to soak until cold. Drain in a sieve,

pressing out surplus liquid. Toss all ingredients together and garnish with watercress.
SERVES 1

VARIATION: Good with turkey, chicken or prawns.
WSP NOTE: Bread allowance exchanged for bulgar wheat.

Tuna Toast Topper   DAY 3 (hot)

3 oz (80 g) tuna in brine
2 teaspoons chopped capers
1 tomato, chopped

½ muffin or 1 oz (25 g) slice
  wholemeal bread
1 teaspoon Parmesan

Mash tuna with brine, capers and tomato. Toast bread or muffin, then pile on tuna topping, dust with Parmesan and grill again until hot. Serve with green salad with a diet dressing.

Tofu Salad   DAY 4 (cold)

¼ cucumber
4 oz (115 g) sliced green beans,
  cooked
3 oz (80 g) soft tofu, diced
1 tablespoon diet French dressing

2 teaspoons lemon juice
1 tomato
Strips of tinned pimento
1 tablespoon snipped chives

Dice half of the cucumber and toss with beans, tofu, dressing and lemon juice. Season to taste. Turn into a dish and top with sliced tomato and the remaining cucumber, sliced. Decorate with strips of pimento and chives. Serve with bread allowance.
SERVES 1

Prawn and Pepper Minestra   DAY 4 (hot)

1 small green pepper, chopped
1 small courgette, sliced
1 clove garlic, crushed
1 stick celery, sliced
2–3 Brussels sprouts, sliced

2 tomatoes, chopped
½ chicken stock cube
½ pint (300 ml) boiling water
3 oz (80 g) prawns
Parmesan cheese

Place vegetables, stock and water in a pan, cover and simmer for 7–10 minutes until tender. Add prawns to the chunky soup and serve dusted with Parmesan cheese and accompany with bread allowance.
SERVES 1

VARIATION: Good with chicken or turkey.

Spring Chicken Salad DAY 5 (cold)

¼ cucumber, sliced thickly
1 head chicory, sliced thickly
2 sticks celery, chopped
3 oz (80 g) cooked chicken, diced
2 teaspoons tarragon vinegar

1 artificial sweetener
1 teaspoon French mustard
2 drops Worcestershire sauce
Freshly ground black pepper

Combine cucumber, chicory, celery and chicken. Mix together remaining ingredients to make a dressing. Pour dressing over the salad and mix well. Serve with bread allowance.
SERVES 1

Chinese Chicken Sweet and Sour DAY 5 (hot)

1 small packet bean sprouts
4 oz (115 g) mushrooms, sliced
3 oz (80 g) cooked chicken, diced
1 teaspoon vinegar

1 artificial sweetener
3 tablespoons soy sauce
¾ oz (20 g) rice, cooked

Heat frying pan and briskly stir-fry all ingredients together for 3–5 minutes.
SERVES 1

VARIATION: Good with turkey or prawns.
WSP NOTE: Bread allowance is exchanged for rice.

DINNER RECIPES

Italian Baked Fish
DAY 1 (a)

4 oz (115 g) frozen peas
11 oz (325 g) white fish fillets (cod, haddock or plaice)
2 teaspoons lemon juice
2 teaspoons Italian mixed herbs

Salt and pepper
1 green pepper, diced
1 small head fennel, sliced thinly
4 tomatoes, sliced

Place fish in baking dish and top with remaining ingredients, finishing with layer of tomatoes. Bake for 25–30 minutes at 350°F, 180°C, Gas mark 4.
SERVES 2

Grilled Fish
DAY 1 (b)

11 oz (325 g) white fish cutlets or steaks (cod, haddock) or whole fish (sole, plaice, heads removed)
4 tablespoons milk or yogurt
3 teaspoons grated Parmesan
Freshly ground black pepper

Marinate fish in milk, Parmesan and seasoning for 2 hours before grilling. Serve with boiled cucumber and peas.
SERVES 2

Liver and Kidney Kebabs
DAY 2 (a)

4 oz (115 g) lamb's liver
2 lamb's kidneys
8 pickling onions
4 tomatoes

1 green pepper
6 bay leaves
4 teaspoons lemon juice
Salt and pepper

Cut the liver into large dice and quarter the kidneys. Boil the onions for 2 minutes, halve the tomatoes and cut the pepper into 8. Thread the ingredients on skewers, sprinkle with lemon juice and season before grilling. Serve with a green salad.
SERVES 2

WSP NOTE: Exchange half day's portion of liver for kidneys.

Liver and Onion Casserole DAY 2 (b)

8 oz (225 g) lamb's liver
2 onions, sliced
2 sticks celery, sliced
1 chicken stock cube

1 glass dry red wine
½ wine glass water
1 teaspoon sage
Salt and pepper

Cut the liver into slices. Cook the remaining items in an uncovered pan and boil for 1 minute. Add liver, then cover and simmer gently for 10 minutes. Serve with carrots or green beans.
SERVES 2

WSP NOTE: 80% of calorie content of wine is lost in cooking.

Paprika Chicken DAY 3 (a)

2 chicken breasts, raw
1 red pepper, sliced
8 oz (225 g) leeks, sliced
4 tomatoes, sliced

2 tablespoons mild paprika
1 teaspoon Tabasco
Salt and pepper
4 tablespoons yogurt

Skin the chicken joints and place in a casserole with all the remaining ingredients, except the yogurt. Bake for 1 hour at 350°F, 180°C, Gas mark 4. Serve dotted with yogurt and with broccoli or green beans.
SERVES 2

VARIATION: Good with fish and peas, bake for 25 minutes.
WSP NOTE: Yogurt from daily milk allowance.

Baked Chicken and Ginger with Chinese Vegetables DAY 3 (b)

2 chicken breasts, raw
1 tablespoon grated ginger
4 oz (115 g) diced parsnip
1 teaspoon grated orange rind
1 tablespoon lemon juice

Salt and pepper
1 tin mixed Chinese vegetables
2 courgettes, diced
3 tablespoons soy sauce

Make foil parcels of the chicken with ginger, parsnips, orange rind, lemon juice and seasoning. Bake for 45 minutes at 350°F, 180°C, Gas mark 4. Stir-fry the courgettes with Chinese vegetables and soy sauce.
SERVES 2

VARIATION: Good with turkey or white fish.

Veal and Pepper Stew DAY 4 (a)

6 fl oz (170 ml) water
1 packet instant vegetable or chicken bouillon
6 oz (170 g) veal, cut in chunks
1 tablespoon onion flakes
1 green pepper, sliced
Paprika and garlic salt to taste
1 tomato, diced
2 oz (50 g) sweetcorn, drained

Heat water with bouillon. Bring the veal to the boil in the bouillon, and add onion flakes and green pepper and season with paprika and garlic. Add tomato and sweetcorn. Cover and simmer for 1 hour or until the veal is tender.
SERVES 1

Rabbit Casserole DAY 4 (b)

2 rabbit legs
2 fl oz (50 ml) cider vinegar
4 fl oz (115 ml) water
1 bay leaf   1 teaspoon juniper berries
1 teaspoon allspice
Freshly ground black pepper
2 medium carrots, thickly sliced
1 stock cube   Diet jelly jam

Marinate the rabbit in vinegar, water, bay leaf, juniper, allspice and pepper for 1–2 days in the refrigerator. Turn occasionally. Lift out and grill joints until brown, then stew with marinade, sliced carrots, stock cube and diet jelly for 1 hour. Lift out carrot and rabbit and strain juices over the top.
   Serve with sweetcorn and grilled mushrooms if wished.
SERVES 2

VARIATION: Good for skinned chicken joints.

Sukiyaki
DAY 5 (a)

8 oz (225 g) cooked turkey, in chunks
4 oz (115 g) mushrooms, sliced
8 oz (225 g) fresh spinach, torn in pieces
4 sticks celery, sliced

2 onions, sliced
1 artificial sweetener
½ chicken stock cube
5 tablespoons water
3 tablespoons soy sauce

Mix all the ingredients together. Simmer gently until celery is just tender, about 7 minutes. Do not overcook.
SERVES 2

VARIATION: Good with white fish or chicken.

Turkey Curry
DAY 5 (b)

10 oz (280 g) turkey breast
2 teaspoons curry powder
1 nectarine, sliced
2 courgettes or handful of green beans

5 fl oz (150 ml) very low fat yogurt
1 small aubergine, diced
¼ teaspoon ground ginger
1 artificial sweetener

Cut turkey into fingers, mix with remaining ingredients in a saucepan and cook gently for 15–20 minutes or until the turkey is tender.
SERVES 2

VARIATION: Good with chicken.
WSP NOTE: Nectarine and yogurt are from part of daily allowances.

RECIPES FOR MID-WEEK ENTERTAINING

Company ChickenDAY 3 or 5

Grated rind and juice 1 orange
2 fl oz (50 ml) lemon juice
1 artificial sweetener
1 teaspoon marjoram
1½ lb (675 g) cooked chicken, boned and sliced
1 tablespoon chopped parsley

Combine juices and artificial sweetener. Add orange rind and marjoram. Cook over a low heat for 5 minutes, stirring constantly. Place chicken in a casserole, spoon the sauce over it and bake for 15 minutes at 350°F, 180°C, Gas mark 4.

Garnish with parsley and serve with baked leeks.
SERVES 4

VARIATION: Good with turkey.

Grilled ChickenDAY 3

2½–3 lb (1.1–1.4 kg) chicken, quartered and skinned
lemon juice
4 celery sticks, sliced
2 tablespoons soy sauce
2 tablespoons tarragon vinegar

Brush chicken with lemon juice and cover with celery strips. Marinate for 1 hour in the remaining ingredients.

Grill on each side for about 20 minutes or until tender, basting occasionally with marinade.

Weigh your diet chicken portion without skin or bones.
SERVES 4

Casserole of Chicken in a Slow CookerDAY 3, 4 or 5

4 chicken breasts, without skin
4 mugs of any mix of chopped celery, broccoli and green pepper
2 mugs of any mix of chopped tomatoes, carrots and onions

Put all the vegetables into the slow cooker and place the chicken over them. Mix sauce ingredients together (see below) and bring to the boil. Pour over the chicken, cover and cook for 6–8 hours on low setting.

Sauce 1
Salt, pepper, rosemary leaves, 4 fl oz (115 ml) wine vinegar, 8 fl oz (225 ml) water, 2 artificial sweeteners

Sauce 2
Salt, pepper, paprika, garlic powder, 1 teaspoon oregano, 3 tablespoons lemon juice, 8 fl oz (225 ml) water.
SERVES 4

VARIATION: Good with chicken or rabbit.

Baked Italian Chicken   DAY 3 or 5

4 chicken breasts, halved and skin removed
Salt and pepper to taste
2 teaspoons Italian mixed herbs
2 cloves crushed garlic
1 glass wine
4 fl oz (115 ml) water
2 aubergines, sliced

Place the chicken pieces in a baking dish. Combine remaining ingredients and pour over the chicken. Bake at 350°F, 180°C, Gas mark 4, for 1 hour.
SERVES 4

VARIATION: Good with turkey.

Chicken Liver Pâté   DAY 2

1 lb (450 g) chicken livers
1 artificial sweetener
2 sticks celery, sliced
6 tomatoes, scalded and peeled
1 teaspoon vinegar

Wash chicken livers thoroughly, make sure all pieces of fat are removed. Combine all ingredients and simmer until celery and livers are tender and well reduced. Mash or purée to a paste.

Serve with melba toast and a mixed green salad tossed in diet dressing.
SERVES 3

Curried Veal
DAY 4, 3, or 5

1½ lb (675 g) veal, cut up
1 orange, peeled and chopped
2 cloves garlic, sliced
2 stock cubes
¼ teaspoon ginger

1 aubergine, diced
1 artificial sweetener
1 tablespoon curry powder
5 fl oz (150 ml) very low fat yogurt

Brown veal in a non-stick pan. Add remaining ingredients and cook on a low heat until veal is tender. Add a little water if needed.
SERVES 4

VARIATION: Good with chicken or turkey.
WSP NOTE: Orange and yogurt are from part of daily allowance.

Sweet-and-Sour Veal
DAY 4

1½ lb (675 g) minced veal
2 tablespoons Worcestershire sauce
1 tablespoon prepared mustard
1 tablespoon soy sauce
6 fl oz (170 ml) water
1 chicken or beef stock cube

4 orange slices
1 large or 2 small green peppers, cut into chunks
14 oz (400 g) tin unsweetened pineapple chunks
2 packets bean sprouts

Combine the minced veal with the Worcestershire sauce, mustard and soy sauce. Mix thoroughly and shape into 12 balls. Heat the water and add the stock cube. Put the meatballs in bouillon and add the remaining ingredients, except the bean sprouts. Simmer for 20–30 minutes or until done. Add bean sprouts, cook for 1 or 2 minutes and serve.
SERVES 4

WSP NOTE: Fruit from daily allowance.

Hunger

You may experience some hunger on the WSP. This is quite natural. Hunger is the signal that your body is running on a calorie deficit and is therefore burning up your extra body fat to obtain needed energy. What you are feeling here is yourself losing weight. Think of it that way and turn it into a good feeling.

Most people find that a mid-morning or afternoon cup of coffee stimulates the sense of hunger, and pangs are felt shortly after. Learn to recognise your own reactions and reserve coffee for just after meals if it weakens your resolve.

True hunger pangs last for only twenty minutes. If you distract yourself for this amount of time, your hunger will be gone and you will be comfortable again.

Have courage. Each time you experience hunger and decide to respond by not eating, you are training your body to learn new responses. Nobody has ever starved to death in twenty minutes. Hunger does not mean you have to eat. Here's what you can do instead of eating when hunger pangs strike. See what you can add to this list:

- Take a brisk walk in the fresh air.
- Exercise your green fingers and prune, root, water and feed your plants.
- Prepare a large tumbler of water, ice and a twist of lemon. Sip slowly with a straw.
- Play with children and/or pets (yours or somebody else's).
- Enjoy a long, hot bath with bath oil or bubbles for an extra treat.
- Write a letter to a friend.
- Run up and down the stairs until you need a rest.
- Call a dieting friend or a positive-thinking one.
- Gargle with mouthwash.
- Make a list of nice, pleasant happy things in your life.
- Pray.
- Knit, crochet, or sew small projects, so you can enjoy the satisfaction of finishing them.
- Buy a magazine, curl up and enjoy it from cover to cover.

- Reach for your mate instead of your plate.
- Relax with a soothing warm drink.
- Talk on the 'phone with a friend (use any extension but the one in the kitchen).
- Brush your teeth.
- Make a list of little jobs you can accomplish in five or ten minutes (you'll be amazed at how many there are), and then do them. Cross each one off as you finish it.
- Turn the radio up high and scream.
- Manicure your nails.
- Go shopping and treat yourself to something fun (facial), luxurious (perfume), pretty (scarf), or extra (fancy writing paper).
- Plant bulbs or seeds, mow grass, rake leaves.
- Take your dog for a walk.
- Put on a record and dance.
- Read a book.
- Go swimming.
- Cry.
- Kick a pillow around the house.
- Wash and blow dry your hair.
- Think thin.
- Exercise.
- Run through your yoga or slimnastic routines.
- When all else fails, look in a three-way mirror.

What weight?

This sounds like such a simple question. However, many people are never quite sure what they should weigh.

They may find out that a person whose figure they admire weighs 130 pounds (58.9 kg) for example, and then they figure that's how much they should weigh. Or some people may read in a magazine or newspaper that if your height is *x*, then you should weigh *y*. These two examples certainly provide some guidelines, but are they right for *you*?

As with many other important questions we encounter in life for which we would like neat black-and-white answers, all we

METROPOLITAN HEIGHT & WEIGHT TABLES

WOMEN

HEIGHT Feet	Inches	m	WEIGHT lb Small Frame	kg	lb Medium Frame	kg	lb Large Frame	kg
4	10	1.47	102–111	46.3–50.3	109–121	49.4–54.9	118–131	53.5–59.4
4	11	1.50	103–113	46.7–51.3	111–123	50.3–55.8	120–134	54.5–60.8
5	0	1.52	104–115	47.2–52.2	113–126	51.3–57.2	122–137	55.3–62.1
5	1	1.55	106–118	48.1–53.5	115–129	52.2–58.5	125–140	56.7–63.5
5	2	1.57	108–121	49.0–54.9	118–132	53.5–59.9	128–143	58.1–64.9
5	3	1.60	111–124	50.3–56.2	121–135	54.9–61.2	131–147	59.4–66.7
5	4	1.63	114–127	51.7–57.6	124–138	56.2–62.6	134–151	60.7–68.5
5	5	1.65	117–130	53.0–59.0	127–141	57.6–64.0	137–155	62.1–70.3
5	6	1.68	120–133	54.4–60.3	130–144	59.0–65.3	140–159	63.5–72.1
5	7	1.70	123–136	55.7–61.7	133–147	60.3–66.7	143–163	64.7–73.9
5	8	1.73	126–139	57.2–63.0	136–150	61.7–68.0	146–167	66.2–75.7
5	9	1.75	129–142	58.5–64.4	139–153	63.0–69.4	149–170	67.6–77.1
5	10	1.78	132–145	59.9–65.8	142–156	64.4–70.8	152–173	68.9–78.5
5	11	1.80	135–148	61.2–67.1	145–159	65.8–72.1	155–176	70.3–79.8
6	0	1.83	138–151	62.6–68.5	148–162	67.1–73.5	158–179	71.7–81.1

MEN

HEIGHT Feet Inches	m	lb Small Frame kg	lb Medium Frame kg	lb Large Frame kg
5 2	1.57	128–134 58.1–60.8	131–141 59.4–64.0	138–150 62.6–68.0
5 3	1.60	130–136 58.9–61.6	133–143 60.3–64.8	140–153 63.5–69.3
5 4	1.63	132–138 59.8–62.6	135–145 61.2–65.8	142–156 64.4–70.8
5 5	1.65	134–140 60.7–63.5	137–148 62.1–67.1	144–160 65.3–72.6
5 6	1.68	136–142 61.7–64.4	139–151 63.0–68.5	146–164 66.2–74.2
5 7	1.70	138–145 62.6–65.7	142–154 64.4–69.9	149–168 67.5–76.1
5 8	1.73	140–148 63.5–67.1	145–157 65.8–71.2	152–172 68.9–78.0
5 9	1.75	142–151 64.4–68.5	148–160 67.1–72.6	155–176 70.3–79.9
5 10	1.78	144–154 65.3–69.9	151–163 68.4–73.9	158–180 71.7–81.6
5 11	1.80	146–157 66.2–71.2	154–166 69.8–75.2	161–184 73.0–83.5
6 0	1.83	149–160 67.5–72.6	157–170 71.2–77.1	164–188 74.4–85.2
6 1	1.85	152–164 68.9–74.4	160–174 72.6–78.9	168–192 76.2–87.1
6 2	1.88	155–168 70.3–76.2	164–178 74.4–80.7	172–197 78.0–89.4
6 3	1.90	158–172 71.7–78.0	167–182 75.7–82.7	176–202 79.9–91.6
6 4	1.93	162–176 73.5–79.9	171–187 77.6–84.4	181–207 90.0–93.8

can offer is a range of grey – there is no number we can give you that is exactly right for you.

On the previous pages are the latest Metropolitan Life Insurance Company Height and Weight Tables. These tables are based on the 1979 Build Study, Society of Actuaries and Association of Life Insurance Medical Directors of America, 1980. The weights include wearing indoor clothing, and also include women wearing shoes with 1-inch heels.

What is good about the Metropolitan tables is that you can choose from a broad choice of 'what's right' according to the actuarial criterion of how long people live. What that means is that people live longer at these weights.

The following weight chart is what The Diet Workshop recommends to its members. These charts were created by Norman Joliffe, M.D., the New York doctor who created the idea of losing weight by eating a balanced diet. These charts assume both men and women are wearing indoor clothing but no shoes.

You may not want to be the weight indicated on any table or chart. It's your choice. Be the weight you want to be. Be the weight that feels best for you. Not everyone is meant to be a Twiggy. You'll be at your ideal weight when you can look in the mirror, turn yourself all the way around, and smile and say 'you look great,' or even, 'I can live with this!'

Goals

All that said and done, it's important to set that goal *now* so that when you get there, you'll know that you've arrived! So, before you even start The Wild Weekend Diet, decide what you want to weigh. Think back to when you looked and felt your best. Even if that was twenty years ago, you can weigh that weight and feel that good again.

There is nothing wrong with interim goals either. Some people feel motivated best by short-term goals. If you want to lose ten pounds before you determine just what your long-term weight will be, that's okay, too.

THE DIET WORKSHOP® WEIGHT CHART

WOMEN

HEIGHT Feet	Inches	m	Small Frame lb	kg	Medium Frame lb	kg	Large Frame lb	kg
4	10	1.47	108	49.0	116	52.6	124	56.2
4	11	1.50	110	49.8	118	53.5	126	57.1
5	0	1.52	113	51.3	121	54.9	129	58.5
5	1	1.55	116	52.6	124	56.2	132	59.8
5	2	1.57	120	54.4	128	58.1	136	61.7
5	3	1.60	123	55.8	132	59.9	140	63.5
5	4	1.63	127	57.6	136	61.7	144	65.3
5	5	1.65	130	59.0	139	63.0	148	67.1
5	6	1.68	134	60.8	142	64.4	152	68.9
5	7	1.70	138	62.6	146	66.2	156	70.8
5	8	1.73	142	64.4	150	68.0	160	72.6
5	9	1.75	146	66.2	154	69.9	163	73.9
5	10	1.78	150	68.0	158	71.7	166	75.2
5	11	1.80	154	69.9	162	73.5	170	77.1
6	0	1.83	158	71.7	166	75.2	174	78.9

MEN

HEIGHT Feet	Inches	m	Small Frame lb	kg	Medium Frame lb	kg	Large Frame lb	kg
5	0	1.52	118	53.5	126	57.2	134	60.8
5	1	1.55	121	54.9	129	58.5	137	52.1
5	2	1.57	124	56.2	132	59.8	140	63.5
5	3	1.60	127	57.6	135	61.2	143	64.8
5	4	1.63	131	59.4	139	63.0	147	66.6
5	5	1.65	134	60.8	142	64.4	150	68.0
5	6	1.68	138	62.6	146	66.2	154	69.9
5	7	1.70	142	64.4	150	68.0	158	71.7
5	8	1.73	145	65.7	154	69.9	162	73.5
5	9	1.75	150	68.0	158	71.7	166	75.2
5	10	1.78	154	69.9	162	73.5	170	77.1
5	11	1.80	158	71.7	166	75.2	176	79.9
6	0	1.83	164	74.4	172	78.1	182	82.7
6	1	1.85	170	77.1	178	80.1	188	85.2
6	2	1.88	178	80.7	184	83.5	194	88.0
6	3	1.90	184	83.6	190	86.2	200	90.7

The idea is to set a goal, be it your final number or a definite number of pounds. Choose what feels best to you. But *choose*. And just so you won't forget your goal, write it down on the title page of this book. NOW.

Goal range

I created the principle of Goal Range to deal with the maddening imprecision of the weight-loss process, to lessen the frustration of looking at a scale that goes up and, sometimes, down, for no particular reason that you can determine.

The Goal Range simply says that, instead of demanding of yourself that you weigh in at one particular weight each day, you choose a range of pounds that is okay with you.

So, for instance, if your Goal Weight is 110 pounds (49.8 kg), as is mine, according to The Diet Workshop Chart for a 4'11" (1.49 m) person, dressed, small frame, I consider my weight to be fine if I weigh between 110 pounds (49.8 kg) and 112 pounds (50.8 kg). In general, women, especially women 5'4" (1.62 m) and under, should limit their range to 2 pounds (1 kg), taller women and men may elect a 3 pound (1.5 kg) range.

Choose your range now. Add it to the number you've inscribed on the title page as your goal.

You will be happily surprised, relieved and delighted at the comfort you will derive in your life *après* dieting by using a Goal Range to live within rather than working at the impossible task of being at the exact same weight every day.

Weighing in

How many times have you gone on a diet, weighed yourself at the very beginning (probably groaned at the number you saw!), and then begun the ritual of 'hopping on and off the scales' every other minute? Do you remember the discouragement you felt when the scale did not register at the exact number you expected? On The Wild Weekend Diet it is very important not to weigh yourself constantly (by constantly we mean morning, noon and night, seven days a week).

Give yourself a break – give your body the time it needs to show a true weight loss. People who get up every morning and head straight for the scales are often in for disappointment. Certainly your true weight is in the morning, before you eat or drink anything, and without clothing. So weigh yourself when you begin the diet, today! Then weigh yourself on Saturday mornings once a week, using the same scales each time, and if it is the spring-type, be sure that it is adjusted to the same place each time. Saturday is the best day because you will see the results of the Weekday Slimdown Plan (WSP) as weight loss on the scales. You will then enjoy The Wild Weekend you have earned. *Do not weigh yourself on Monday!* You may get the urge – but resist it!

Questions and answers

Question: I hate to be told what to eat, let alone when to eat it. Do I have to follow the WSP in order? May I mix and match the days?
Answer: You may exchange any one whole day's plan for another. Each day on the WSP is equal in calories to all the others. You may even eat the same foods every day. However, for nutrition insurance, we recommend you eat a wide variety of foods on the WSP.

Question: I'm working the night shift and always eating on a different schedule from my family. Can I eat the dinner meal at lunchtime and the lunch meal at dinner time?
Answer: Yes. You may arrange your daily meals in any order that fits into your particular lifestyle. Just be sure to limit your eating to those foods recommended for any given day.

Question: Even though I have been dieting for several years, I still have trouble choosing restaurants that fit my diet. Help me, please!
Answer: Not every restaurant will fit your diet. You'll have most trouble in ethnic restaurants and fast-food places without salad bars. Telephone the restaurant first and ask if they have a salad bar or serve grilled fish or poultry. Plan WSP restaurant eating

ahead of time – do not wait until you arrive hungry, when you are most likely to eat whatever they serve.

NB Don't hesitate about calling the restaurant. They would rather hear from you and get your business than have you worry and stay away. And they're used to getting calls. People whose health depends on what they eat, such as people with diabetes, ulcers, colitis, and other digestive diseases, allergies and other problems, call because the penalty of eating the wrong foods is more long-lasting than the temporary discomfort of making the call.

Question: I can't eat grapefruit or oranges. They give me migraine. You require a citrus fruit every day. Is there something I can eat instead?
Answer: Yes, you can substitute 8 fluid ounces (225 ml) of tomato juice for these fruits. Tomatoes and tomato juice are high in vitamin C, as are the citrus fruits. Anyone allergic to other foods on the diet should turn to the Core Diet on page 165 and look for similar foods from the same group.

Question: I've read a lot about dieting and the effects of caffeine, but I really like the taste of real coffee. Do I have to give up my 'cuppa' on this diet?
Answer: Caffeine is a drug found in all coffee and most teas. For the dieter, a cup of coffee has historically been used as a hunger chaser. In reality the caffeine in the coffee and tea stimulates the production of insulin into the bloodstream, which sets off a feeling of hunger. You are better off drinking decaffeinated coffee and tea and diet beverages as much as possible. However, one or two cups of real coffee per day is acceptable, particularly after meals.

Question: I am really a very thirsty person. I drink about 5 pints (3 litres) of liquid a day. May I drink as many fizzy diet drinks as I like?
Answer: A word of caution. Many of the diet drinks are sweetened with sodium saccharin, excessive use of which may cause bloating (water retention), and this will be bad for your health, weight and may increase your thirst. Look for diet

drinks sweetened with aspartame (Nutra Sweet). It is good for everyone to drink at least 3 pints (2 litres) of liquid a day. It is more thirst quenching and better for your health to drink plenty of water. If tap water is unacceptable, drink bottled water such as Evian, Vichy or Perrier.

Question: I am what you might call a compulsive nibbler. When I am dieting, I need to snack on raw vegetables in the middle of the afternoon or I look for biscuits. Can I do this on the WSP?
Answer: Plan for an alternative to an afternoon snack habit. Try drinking hot beverages or a diet drink, or take a walk instead. If all else fails, eat a salad made of lettuce, cucumber and tomatoes.
NB: If you are following the WSP as directed, you probably won't experience much hunger in the middle of the afternoon.

Question: Not a week goes by that I don't have at least one social event or business function to go to. If I start the WSP on Monday and have to eat a high-calorie meal at a banquet or business dinner on Wednesday, will I blow my diet?
Answer: You don't 'have' to eat a high-calorie meal on Wednesday, regardless of where you might be. Look closely at the meal and eat only the foods that fit into your diet plan for that day. If there are none, eat the salad (ask for a double without dressing), order plenty of soda water and decaffeinated coffee, and eat your meal when you get home. Remember, the success of the diet depends on following the WSP exactly as written. Hang on in there! The Wild Weekend is coming!

Question: Believe it or not, I sometimes don't want to eat as much as my food plan allows. If I eat less one day during the week, can I add the balance of that day's menu to the next day's menu?
Answer: No. If you don't eat all the foods recommended on any given day, forget them and follow the next day's plan exactly as it is written with no additions.

Question: I have a vegetable garden, and growing tomatoes is my speciality. However, I am not crazy about eating raw vegetables. I notice that you permit tomatoes to be eaten as desired

in a salad for lunch and dinner. May I eat tomatoes, cooked as desired?
Answer: Yes. You may eat as many tomatoes as you want, cooked or raw. Remember green beans, peppers, cucumber, courgettes and all green salads are free vegetables so plant an interesting variety of these if you are a keen gardener. Just make sure you don't create a glut of new potatoes and fall for these!

Question: I enjoy eggs for breakfast, but if I can't fry them in butter, they seem dry and rubbery. Any suggestions?
Answer: You may use a non-stick spray to fry or scramble your eggs. Or, if you like a moister egg, try poaching it in boiling water, tomato juice, V-8 juice, or bouillon.

Question: I know I have to give up my sauces and gravies while I am on the WSP, but do I have to give up flavour altogether?
Answer: Absolutely not. Use a variety of herbs, spices and seasonings. You will not be giving up flavour – just calories. Try new combinations: dill or rosemary on chicken; garlic powder and a sprinkle of vinegar on turkey; a little grated Parmesan cheese on fish; and use parsley and paprika to 'dress up' your entrées.

Question: Lemon is listed in the extras section of the WSP. How can I use it?
Answer: Use lemons and limes to flavour and enhance your meals. Sprinkle them on fresh vegetables, fish and chicken. Fresh or bottled lemon may be used to make lemonade. Sweeten it with artificial sweetener. Spice up your tea with a fresh lemon wedge and make a refreshing summer cooler with sparkling water and fresh lemon or lime (or both) wedges.

Question: My husband and I have a pre-dinner drink every day. He doesn't like it when I don't join him. What can I do while on the WSP?
Answer: First of all, you make the drinks. Give him his usual, and give yourself some sparkling water perked up with lemon or lime. Or, use your fruit allowance, and make yourself a Virgin Mary – a tomato juice with Worcestershire sauce only. Join him socially, but save the alcohol calories for the weekend.

Question: The supermarkets are flooded now with all brands of low-calorie margarines. Is it allowed on the WSP for breakfast toast?
Answer: No fats, butter or margarine are permitted on the WSP. Even though the new low-calorie brands do save you calories, they will still add extra, non-nutritional calories to your WSP. Use diet jam to moisten and sweeten your breakfast toast.

Question: My sister is on The Wild Weekend Diet. She says she doesn't have to eat all the foods on the WSP. She says she will lose faster if she doesn't. Is this true?
Answer: No, she probably will not lose weight faster and, in the process, will harm herself by eating less than is recommended on the WSP. There are not a lot of calories on the mid-week diet and the foods recommended are packed with nutritional value. If there appears to be too much food for her, advise her to cut back on the amount of salad she is eating and concentrate on the vegetables and chicken, fish and other protein. It is vital that these are eaten or your health will suffer.

Question: The Wild Weekend Diet is the best diet I have ever seen. You allow two breads per day on the WSP. (Some diets I have been on don't allow any bread, and I am a breadaholic!) What kinds of breads may I have on the WSP?
Answer: Any bread that has no fruit or nuts in it is permitted. You may select from white, wholewheat, rye, pumpernickel, wholemeal rolls or baps, muffins, pitta bread in 1 oz (25 g) servings two times daily. Avoid the raisin, banana and date-nut breads until the Wild Weekend. We are glad you think The Wild Weekend Diet is the best; we do, too!

Question: My teenage daughter needs to lose weight. I would like her to go on this diet with me, but there don't seem to be enough calories for her on the WSP. What do you suggest for teenagers on the WSP?
Answer: Teenagers can go on The Wild Weekend Diet very safely. Teenage bodies are still growing and developing and, therefore, require more calories daily than the mature adult. As a result we have a specially adapted diet for teenagers. Since

they need more calories daily, we allocate them fewer WWUs on their Wild Weekends to ensure their good health as well as success in dieting. See page 50.

Question: As soon as I decide to lose weight, I become a 'scale hopper'. Sometimes I weigh myself four or five times a day. Often I am disappointed, even though I have followed my diet to the letter. How often should I weigh myself?
Answer: Once a week is recommended. Your body's weight changes daily (and many times during the same day) for many reasons. To measure weight loss accurately, you need to weigh yourself on the same scales, at the same time, on the same day of each week. Avoid that temptation to weigh yourself every day to measure your success. Instead, measure your success by acknowledging all the changes you are making in your daily eating habits.

Question: I have high blood pressure and have to take medication to control it. Because of this medication, my doctor told me to eat a banana and drink 8 fluid ounces (225 ml) of orange juice every day. He told me never to omit these. What can I do on the WSP?
Answer: Follow your doctor's advice and eat the banana and drink the orange juice every day. If you consider these as your total fruit intake for the day, they will not interfere with your weight loss.

Question: I have a problem with constipation and varicose veins and my doctor has advised me to eat plenty of high bran cereals and wholemeal bread. He told me to have these every day. What can I do on the WSP?
Answer: Follow your doctor's advice and start your day with a high bran breakfast cereal daily. Have ¾ oz (20 g) All Bran or Bran Buds or bran with part of your milk allowance. At lunch you are allowed 1 oz (25 g) bread, so choose high bran bread. The diet includes peas and sweetcorn, pears, berries and currants, and all are good sources of fibre. Take plenty of high fibre free vegetables like spinach, broccoli, spring greens, green beans, sprouts, mushrooms. If you need to take more bran, stir

it into cottage cheese, or sprinkle it on fish or poultry with a little Parmesan for flavour before grilling or baking instead of your bread allowance.

Question: I live with a very thin husband and three skinny teenagers! When they are munching on biscuits, sweets and snacks I feel very left out. I really don't want to learn to do without this family snack time. What do you suggest?

Answer: They may be thin, but that doesn't mean your family *should* be tucking into biscuits, sweets and snacks daily! There are other aspects of their basic health to consider, plus their teeth and complexions. Save yourself a piece of fruit to eat at this time, and put out a bowl of fruits for the family too, so you can enjoy these together. Try to wean the family off sweets and commercial snacks and on to nuts, raisins and good fresh bread, tea cakes, fruit loaves (not doughnuts or cakes). These you can only enjoy at the weekend on your WWUs. Other lovely summer ideas are to make real fruit juice lolly ices for all the family or make lollies of diet fizzy drinks. Try chopping up your fruit allowance and putting a toothpick in each piece, then freeze for longer lasting crunch nibbles.

· CHAPTER FIVE ·

EATING OUT ON A WILD WEEKEND

When a man or a woman is unfaithful to his or her diet, the most frequently named co-respondent is that villain Eating Out. Sit down at a table that is not your own, and the temptation, the agonised choices, the exotic preparations, the convivial atmosphere, all play a part in doing the diet in. The Wild Weekend Diet is designed to position you for success. In this chapter we will acquaint you with the hazards of restaurant eating and entertaining, tell you how to meet and jump over the hurdles, and show you how to make choices that fit into your Wild Weekend Unit allowance.

Dress for success

Just as you need a special outfit for your evening out, you also need to prepare yourself for your 'holiday from dieting' in order to protect your weight loss.

Start talking to yourself early in the day. Talk about breakfast and lunch. Use these messages to overcome your temptation to skip your No-Think breakfast and lunch. Convince yourself that skipping meals and 'saving' calories is harmful to the health of your diet. Your body needs energy to keep on going and to burn up your fat.

Think positively. Tell yourself that you can do it, that you can stick to your WWU budget, and that you'll enjoy yourself at the same time.

We all have willpower. Some of us will ourselves to stay on

our diet while others of us will ourselves off our diet or to lose the diet battle. But you can be a winner. Think about what you're getting in terms of your choice of wonderful foods to eat, and don't dwell on the fact that you have to practise some restraint and control. When you assert yourself to yourself, you have the power to reach all your goals.

There's more that you can do to get ready for the high point of the diet week. Decide in advance what you'll eat. This is easy if you're going to a familiar restaurant. You know the menu, so you can zero in on what you'll order from soup through to the dessert. For an evening out in an unfamiliar setting you can make some preliminary decisions on how you will spend your WWUs. Will it be in drinks? How many? Or will you go for a sumptuous entrée or a fabulous dessert?

If you take the time and make the effort to think about the meal before the moment of truth, your success is guaranteed!

Temptations abound

The lure of the restaurant assails all your senses. At the door you're greeted by and surrounded with the aromas of all the foods you love. Bountiful trays of beautifully prepared food fill your eyes. From the moment you step into the room you're involved in the eating experience.

Eating possibilities raise their tempting heads the minute you sit down. Special breads and crisp breadsticks – and butter, their trusty sidekick – are within your reach. You already know it's okay to eat what you want on The Wild Weekend Diet, as long as you count WWUs as you munch along. As you order your drink, keep adding your WWUs. If your addition is poor, you don't flunk; you just get left behind, stuck at a weight place you don't like.

Temptations abound at the dinner table. The bread basket is bottomless. Others offer you a bite of this or that, and then there's dessert. Ah, dessert! As long as these samples and tastes appear in your total count, that's fine. Let it be your maxim that 'I will be led into temptation, and I will give in to temptation as long as I count the food in my WWU total, even if I eat only a forkful, *and* as long as I am within my WWU budget.' Everything that passes your lips must pass your scrutiny. Every forkful counts – and must be counted!

Eating out in a restaurant

The arrival of the menu is another test of your commitment. Here's where you exercise your freedom of choice as you balance the foods you want against the WWUs you have to spend. Now figure out the total from pre-dinner drinks, through to dessert, so that you'll enjoy the whole experience in comfort, knowing that you're staying within the limits you have set for yourself.

Expect that each and every food you eat in a restaurant has added calories hidden in its preparation. As chefs offer flair and flavour, so also do they offer butter and cream and other ingredients that are hard to determine and therefore difficult to count up. You won't go wrong if you add 2 WWUs just for walking in the door. In fact, you'll be doing your diet and your get-slim plan a big favour.

Here is a glossary of common menu terms. Knowing what they mean will be helpful in ordering and in keeping an accurate count. Particularly high-calorie ingredients are in italics.

MENU GLOSSARY

TERM	MEANING
A la king	Chopped food, primarily chicken or turkey, in *cream* sauce.
A la mode	Dessert topped with *ice cream*.
Al denté	Pasta and vegetables cooked until tender yet firm.
Almondine	Made or served with *almonds* or other *nuts*. Often covered with *cheese sauce*.
Au gratin	Food that's browned in the oven or grilled, topped with *buttered bread crumbs* and *cheese*.

EATING OUT ON A WILD WEEKEND

TERM	MEANING
Au jus	Meat served in its own juice.
Beurre	Butter, in French.
Bourguignonne	Foods prepared in *Burgundy wine sauce*, which usually includes *butter* and *cream*.
Brûlé	Burned, in French. Term used to describe food glazed with caramelised *sugar*.
Café au lait	Coffee with milk or *cream*.
Canapé	Choice of often high fat items on *fried bread*, *rich biscuits* or in *puff pastry*.
Cappucino	Steamed full fat milk with a little espresso coffee added.
Cordon bleu	Filled with *ham* and *cheese*, *crumbed* and *fried*.
Crêpe	A thin pancake.
Croquettes	Food that is coated in *breadcrumbs* and *deep fat fried*.
En brochette	Food that is cooked on a skewer.
En cocotte	Cooked in a casserole.
En croûte	Wrapped in or topped with a *crust*, usually high fat puff pastry.
Flambé	Desserts soaked in *liquor*, often cooked in *butter* and set ablaze.
Fricassee	Poultry that is cooked in *sauce* after being browned in *oil* or *butter*.
Fromage	Cheese, in French.
Julienne	Food cut in thin strips.
Marinated	Foods soaked in a liquid mixture for several hours until the food absorbs the flavour. Often *oil* is part of the marinade or mixture.
Poisson	Fish, in French.
Poulet	Chicken, in French.
Provençale	Dishes that are cooked and served with onion, garlic and *olive oil*.
Ragoût	A hearty stew, in thick *gravy*.
Sautéed	Pan-fried in a small amount of hot *oil* or *butter*.
Suprême	Chicken, turkey or fish in *cream* sauce.

Bigger is not better

It's time to look at some typical restaurant menus and the WWU analysis of each food. But before we do that there is one thing you must be aware of: the portion size served. In Chapter 3, Off For The Weekend, I told you that WWUs are computed on the basis of three criteria: type of food, portion size and method of preparation. Don't give yourself permission to ignore the size of what is served to you. If you want to eat a lot, that's fine as long as you can 'afford' to do so within your total allowance.

Sample menus

Each of the following menus is based on 22 or fewer WWUs. That means that each of the menus would suit a woman's Saturday night Wild Weekend Unit budget, and if you're a man, you still have 7 additional WWUs to spend. These counts were derived by taking the WWU value for each food item in the menu and keeping a running total on the meal. The sources used are the Food Lists in Chapters 7, 8 and 9.

The meals include a world of food choices, and they show you the many different ways you can choose WWUs that suit your taste. You'll find sample menus from Italian restaurants to French bistros, from Greek tavernas to Indian kitchens, as well as from Chinese restaurants and fast-food chains. You may follow these menu plans exactly, or you can use them as examples of what costs what in Wild Weekend Units.

The WWU value for all main courses was worked out as the result of a three-step process:

1. First we took the WWU value for 6 oz (170 g) of cooked meat, fish, poultry, eggs or cheese.
2. To this total we added the WWU value for the method of preparation (Hot List items).
3. Finally we added WWUs for any additions, such as sauces, gravies, creams, stuffing, or cheese or bread toppings (again, Hot List items).

The WWU value for all other courses was calculated by totalling calories found in standard recipes and converting the calories to WWUs based on an average serving.

SAMPLE MENUS FOR SATURDAY NIGHT

FRENCH RESTAURANT (1)	WWUs
White wine, 2 glasses	2
Soupe a l'Oignon	3
French bread, 1 piece	1
Moules Marinière (Mussels with white wine sauce)	3
Sole à la Meunière	4
Creamed Spinach	2
Chocolate mousse	7
Coffee, black	0
	22

FRENCH RESTAURANT (2)	WWUs
Champagne cocktail, 1	3
French garlic bread, 1 slice	3
Beef Bourguignonne	8
Peas, ½ mug	1
Champagne Sorbet	5
Benedictine and Brandy	2
Coffee, black	0
	22

ITALIAN RESTAURANT (1)

	WWUs
Chianti wine, 2 glasses	2
2 Bread sticks	1
Minestrone Soup, 1 mug	3
Tossed salad, with vinegar and lemon	0
Spaghetti Bolognaise	12
Broccoli, cooked in butter	3
Coffee with cream	1
	22

ITALIAN RESTAURANT (2)

	WWUs
Dry Martini, 1	1
White wine, 2 glasses	2
Prosciutto (3 oz/80 g)	3
Lasagna	8
Salad, with oil and vinegar	2
Italian bread, 1 slice, with 1 tablespoon butter	3
Zabaglione	2
Espresso coffee	0
	21

SPANISH RESTAURANT

	WWUs
Sangria, 3 glasses	6
Gaspacho	2
Paella Valencia	10
Salad (no dressing)	0
Mixed ice cream	3
Coffee, white	1
	22

GREEK RESTAURANT (1)

	WWUs
Stuffed vine leaf	2
Hummus, 2 tablespoons	2
Roast leg of lamb with ouzo	8
Pilaf	3
Peas, ½ mug	1
Baklava	5
Coffee, black	0
	21

GREEK RESTAURANT (2)

	WWUs
Beer, light, 12 fl oz (350 ml)	1
Greek salad, with oil and feta	7
Souvlaki	10
Carrots	0
Semolina cake, 2 in (5 cm) square	3
Coffee, black	0
	21

INDIAN RESTAURANT (1)

	WWUs
Lager, 12 fl oz (350 ml)	2
Mulligatawny soup	2
Roghan gosht	8
Raita (cucumber in yoghurt)	1
Poppadom	1
Bindi Bhajee, 1 (Ladies fingers fritter)	2
Pilau rice, ½ mug	2
Onion chutney, 1 tablespoon	1
Chapatti	2
Mango, ½ fresh	1
Coffee, black	0
	22

INDIAN RESTAURANT (2)   WWUs

Shandy, 12 fl oz (350 ml)	1
Samosa, 2	2
Chicken biriany	8
Tarka dhal	4
Obla saag	0
Paratha	4
Guava, ½ mug	2
Tea with lemon	0
	21

CHINESE RESTAURANT (1)   WWUs

White wine, 2 glasses	2
Crispy pancake roll, 1	2
Barbecue spareribs, 2	2
Beef chop suey, ½ mug	2
Sweet sour chicken, ½ mug	3
Egg fried rice, ½ mug	4
King prawn with bamboo shoots, ½ mug	2
Lychees in syrup	2
Tea with lemon	0
	19

CHINESE RESTAURANT (2)   WWUs

White wine, dry, 1 glass	1
Won ton soup	3
Mushroom Foo Yung (1 omelette with sauce)	3
Sweet sour pork in crispy batter, ½ mug	5
Stir-fried beef and vegetables, ½ mug	2

	WWUs
Chicken chow mein	3
Special fried rice	4
Pineapple chunks, ½ mug	1
Tea with lemon	0
	22

BERNI INNS (1)

	WWUs
Gin and tonic	2
Farmhouse grill	10
French beans	0
Jacket potato with butter	4
Salad, no dressing	0
Sorbet sensation (Sorbet blackcurrants and cream)	6
Coffee, black	0
	22

BERNI INNS (2)

	WWUs
Red wine, 2 glasses	2
Steak and butterfly prawns	12
Chips	4
Peas, ½ mug	1
Salad, with dressing	2
Coffee with cream	1
	22

BERNI INNS (3)

	WWUs
Whisky, 1 glass	1
Red wine, 1 glass	1
Soup of the day	2
Roll and butter	3
Rump steak, 5 oz (140 g), grilled	4
Mushrooms, fried	1
Jacket potato and sour cream	4
Salad without dressing	0
Ice cream sundae	5
	21

STEAK HOUSE (1)

	WWUs
Real ale, ½ pint (300 ml)	2
Rump steak, 8 oz (225 g), fried	12
Salad and small chips	8
Black coffee	0
	22

STEAK HOUSE (2)

	WWUs
Whisky and water	1
Grilled gammon, 8 oz (225 g), and 3 slices pineapple	8
Jacket potato and butter	6
Peas, ½ mug	1
Fruit cocktail and ice cream	4
Coffee with cream and sugar	1
	21

WIMPY

	WWUs
Shandy	4
Wimpy Special Grill	9
Apple pie	5
Thick shake	4
	22

PIZZA EXPRESS

	WWUs
1 glass white wine	1
Pizza Capricciosa	12
Extra cheese	2
Bombe	3
Espresso coffee with sugar	2
	20

WENDY'S

	WWUs
Salad bar, 1 platter, full choice of all items, with 2 tablespoons Italian dressing	5
Triple Cheeseburger	12
French fries, regular	4
Diet soda	0
	21

McDONALD'S

	WWUs
Quarter pounder with cheese	7
French fries, regular	4
Hot cakes with butter and syrup	6
Vanilla milk shake	5
	22

KENTUCKY FRIED CHICKEN

	WWUs
Coca Cola	2
Colonel's dinner (2 crispy chicken pieces, chips, coleslaw)	12
Sweetcorn	4
Coffee, white	1
	19

FISH AND CHIP SHOP

	WWUs
Coca Cola	2
Plaice, fried, 7 oz (200 g)	8
Chips, large portion, 12 oz (350 g)	13
Vinegar	0
	23

JEWISH DELICATESSEN

	WWUs
Bagel, 2	8
Cream cheese, ¼ mug	5
Smoked salmon, 4 oz (115 g)	5
Coleslaw, ½ mug	2
Coffee, black	0
	20

COFFEE SHOP

	WWUs
Cream of tomato soup	2
Welsh rarebit and poached egg	9
Green salad, no dressing	0
Potato crisps, 1 oz (25 g)	2

Chocolate éclair	3
Strawberry milk shake	4
	20

MEXICAN — WWUs

Margarita, 1	2
Guacamole dip, ½ mug	3
Tortilla chips, 2 oz (50 g)	4
Burrito	5
Refried beans, ½ mug	3
Flan (caramel custard)	4
Coffee, black	0
	21

PUB FOOD (1) — WWUs

Beaujolais, 2 glasses	2
Steak and kidney pie	15
Carrots	0
Mashed potato, ½ mug	2
White coffee	1
	20

PUB FOOD (2) — WWUs

Draught beer or cider, 1 pint (600 ml)	4
Cornish pastie, large	13
Peas	1
Meringue	4
	22

BUFFET – COLD	WWUs
Champagne, 1 glass	1
Tossed salad (pre-dressed)	3
Roll, small, with butter	3
Roast beef, 1 oz (25 g) slice	2
Tongue, 1 slice, 1 oz (25 g)	2
Salmon salad, ¼ mug	1
Coleslaw, ½ mug	2
Potato salad, ½ mug	3
Trifle, ¾ mug	4
Coffee with cream and sugar	1
	22

BUFFET – HOT	WWUs
Burgundy, 2 glasses	2
Mushroom vol-au-vent	3
Beef curry, ¾ mug	4
Rice, ½ mug	1
Chutney	1
Peas	1
Chicken drumstick, 1	3
Black cherry cheesecake	4
Coffee with cream	1
	20

SAMPLE MENUS FOR SUNDAY LUNCH

Sunday lunch is your second opportunity of the weekend to embark on a food adventure. If you are a woman you have 13 WWUs to spend on lunch; if you are a man you have 15.

If you're asking yourself whether you will lose weight if you spend these extra WWUs on a Sunday lunch, the answer is, 'Yes, you will'. You have saved WWUs all week long which can be spent on your Wild Weekend!

EATING OUT ON A WILD WEEKEND

PUB LUNCH (1) — WWUs

3 diet ginger ale	0
Shepherds pie	12
Black coffee	0
	12

PUB LUNCH (2) — WWUs

1 sherry	2
2 glasses burgundy	2
Hot pot	7
Peas	1
White coffee	1
	13

PUB LUNCH (3) — WWUs

Dry white wine, 3 glasses	3
Ploughman's lunch:	
French bread, 3 slices	3
Butter, ½ oz (12 g)	2
Cheese, 3 oz (80 g)	5
Pickled onion	0
Lettuce and tomato	0
	13

HOTEL RESTAURANT LUNCH (1) — WWUs

Tomato juice	1
2 slices turkey breast	4
Gravy, ½ mug from mix	1
Stuffing, 3 tablespoons	2
Cranberry sauce, 1 tablespoon	1

THE WILD WEEKEND DIET

	WWUs
Roast potato, 1	1
Carrots and cauliflower	0
Fresh fruit salad, ½ mug	2
Coffee, black	0
	12

RESTAURANT LUNCH (2)

	WWUs
Orange juice	1
Roast pork, 2 small slices, 4 oz (115 g)	4
Apple sauce	1
Gravy, ½ mug tinned	2
Sprouts and carrots	0
Roast potatoes, 2	2
Lemon sorbet	2
Coffee, white	1
	13

RESTAURANT LUNCH (3)

	WWUs
Perrier water	0
White wine, 2 glasses	2
Roast lamb, 2 slices, 4 oz (115 g)	4
Mint sauce	0
Gravy, ½ mug tinned	2
Spring greens	0
Roast potato, 1	1
Apple pie	4
Coffee, black	0
	13

Restaurant Tips

Here are some tips for eating out from Laura, one of the test dieters who lost weight very well on The Wild Weekend Diet.

'Relax! This diet is going to work for you. Be informed! After you and your friend, lover, or spouse have decided to go out for dinner, choose the restaurant. Take some time during the week and call ahead to find out how they prepare their dishes. If you know in advance that you are going to eat veal parmigiana because it is your favourite Italian food, you can plan your Wild Weekend meal in advance. If you are going to a familiar restaurant and you are not crazy about the way they prepare their main courses, you can have your fish or chicken grilled plain and then splurge on a favourite dessert like Baked Alaska. Use the Weekend Slimdown Plan as your Bible during the week, then you can be comfortable and feel entitled to spend your Wild Weekend units on Saturday night.

'Be flexible! You can change your mind. When you look over the menu, you may have a change of heart and decide you want a totally different meal from the one you planned. This is okay. Just remember the basic rules of adding Wild Weekend Units for cooking methods (Hot List) and that WWU values are for 6 oz (170 g) of cooked meat or poultry. Stay within your WWU budget!

'Remember that you are in control. When you are served a meal, you do not have to eat every bite. Eat only until you are comfortably satisfied. After you have eaten approximately half your meal, stop! Put your fork down and pay attention to how your body feels. Ask yourself if you are still hungry. If the answer is yes, eat half of what is left, then stop again and ask yourself once more if you are hungry. When you no longer want more food, push your plate away from you and ask the waiter to remove it. If you cannot summon the attention of the waiter, do what I do. Sprinkle the remains with lots of pepper and salt or sugar. Who wants to pick at prime rib with sugar on it? Yuk!

'You do not have to sample all the food that is on the table or on someone else's plate. If bread is a problem and it's not part of your Wild Weekend Unit budget, move the basket from your reach, or better yet, ask that it be removed from the table.

'Ask that your salad be served with the dressing on the side. When a salad is served with the dressing already on it, usually it adds up to 4 WWUs. If you have your salad served with the dressing on the side, you can reduce the Wild Weekend Units by using less dressing. Each tablespoon of regular dressing adds 2 WWUs. This same principle applies to the butter and/or sour cream on baked potatoes or vegetables. Request that the butter or sour cream be served on the side so that you make the decision of how much of these accompaniments you eat.

'Now it's time for dessert. Do you really want it, or are you ordering simply because you've got WWUs left over? Sense how your body is feeling. If you aren't really hungry for dessert, skip it and lose weight a little faster.

'If someone tries to coerce you off your diet and tempts you to eat more than you want, a simple statement I use with great effect is, "I'm full!"

'Many restaurants, in an attempt at grace, offer nuts, sweets and other little temptations in dishes with spoons. Before you dive into these little devils, stop and think for a minute. It is not possible to have all your favourites every weekend and lose weight. I learned this lesson very early in my weight-loss process. Make your choices count. Sweets and nuts are outrageously high in calories. The calories and Wild Weekend Units mount up very quickly when you pick at a bowl of mints or at a box of chocolates. Take my advice: Don't stand near the petits fours or nuts. Engage in conversation with friends who are safely removed from the temptations. Stay close to thin friends. The thin friends I mean are those who watch their weight and are successful at it. Imitate them. Look at the little bowls of sweets and nuts as bowls of fat (that's what chocolate and nuts contain, although they are attractively and deliciously packaged, aren't they?). Then imagine lumps of fat sticking out on your hips and thighs.

'Be strong! Control your appetite. Remember your desire to be thin! You can have your favourite main course and your favourite dessert. You can have breads and cocktails. You can have many of the foods you enjoy but you can't have everything. Is this big news? In the perfect world that never was on earth you can have everything. In this world, the one we live in, you must make choices. Make your choice count and lose weight.'

Home entertaining

Whether you are guest or host when you dine in a home, your dieting plans need special thought. Courtesies must be considered as well as your diet, but don't think that these are incompatible. It is just that thought must be given to how your choices may affect those around you.

Being the perfect guest

At a dinner party your meal has been chosen for you. You may ask for small helpings, you may skip the roast potatoes but there are some things which it is not easy to say 'no' to. Be prepared and aware of this. You can say 'no' to the crisps and nuts and say you would hate to spoil your appetite, but to refuse a pre-dinner drink may seem churlish. You can ask if there is a Slimline tonic for your gin, but don't express the request in such a way that your host feels guilty if there isn't any. Remember to sip your drink *slowly*, then your glass won't look as if it needs topping up. Concentrate on the art of conversation not consumption.

How to say 'No' politely

Start counting those WWUs. Just because you may not *feel* that you have complete control, this is no excuse for not counting. You can say 'no' to offers of croûtons with your soup or buttered bread with your starter, also to cheese and biscuits before dessert (a wise precaution if you know your hostess makes scrumptious desserts or if puds are your great weakness). To offers of second helpings or 'Do just try my other pud,' the politest refusal, if you are running out of WWUs, is 'It has all been quite delicious but I am afraid I'm full.' With this comment you are unlikely to receive further persuasion to eat more.

Never say, 'No, I am on a diet,' because from this excuse you will elicit nothing but a little sympathy and a lot of pressure to break it, just this once, from all who are present. Your hostess will feel particularly piqued if you do not choose this one occasion to forget your diet and will feel her hospitality spurned.

If you have accepted her invitation you should have told her about your diet. If you didn't and she has gone to the trouble of preparing a lovely meal, you owe it to her not to be on a strict WSP diet on the night. This is the tremendous advantage of The Wild Weekend Diet – you can always swop a mid-week day for your Saturday if you have a mid-week dinner party. You don't always have to be the 'diet bore' – you can be a perfect guest and, when necessary, say 'No' without causing offence.

Being the perfect hostess

With one third of the population overweight, it is time we separated the concept of being the ideal host from the belief that the perfect host or hostess is someone who virtually force feeds their guests and firmly plies them with too many drinks. Drink-driving laws are discouraging us from the latter. Now we need to consider the former.

- Do provide low calorie drinks for your guests. Put them out on display – Perrier, Vichy water, Slimline tonic – so that guests feel confident to ask for them.
- 'Do have another drink' sounds more like an order than an invitation to guests. Try 'Would you like another drink' so your guests feel free to decline.
- Do provide sticks of celery, carrot and peppers with your snacks, not just nuts and crisps, so that dieters have a choice.
- Do consider your party menu. Don't have too many pastries, high calorie sauces, sugar or drown the whole thing in butter and cream.
- Do serve separate dressings and sauces, and separate butter for bread and vegetables, so that guests can choose to have or to avoid these.

- Do serve a variety of vegetables, some simply cooked with herbs rather than with butter or cream.
- Do serve at least one low calorie dessert. A fruit with a fruit sauce, such as peaches with raspberry purée, pears with blackcurrant or a sorbet, makes a change from fruit salad.

Questions and answers

Question: What is the best advice you can give me before I go out to a restaurant to eat?
Answer: Psyche yourself into believing that you will make choices that are good for you. As soon as you have plans to go to a restaurant tell yourself that you will be able to stick to your Wild Weekend Diet. Keep telling yourself this over and over and over. You can do it! Many others have done it before you. Tell yourself that you have wonderful Wild Weekend Units to spend on the foods of your choice and then begin to decide what it is you wish to eat and drink. There are no restrictions on the choices, but there are guidelines to follow. Re-read Chapter 4, 'Weekend Slimdown Plan' thoroughly to re-acquaint yourself with the overall instructions and tips for Wild Weekends. Memorise them. Then:

1. Choose a restaurant that offers a wide variety of foods. Don't limit yourself to a place that serves only fried foods. You may eat something fried, but then, again, you may want something grilled or baked.
2. Call the restaurant in advance and ask how the food is prepared. Check to see whether all the vegetables are served in butter and if the main courses are served with sauces and gravies. This is especially important for Greek, Italian and French restaurants. Knowing beforehand, you can then plan how many WWUs you will be spending if and when you order these foods. Ask them if they have a salad bar and if they serve diet salad dressing. If they do not, then you can plan to spend WWUs on salad dressing or make the choice of bringing diet dressing from home or eating your salad plain.

3. Use the sample restaurant meal plans earlier in this chapter to map out your menu ahead of time. Then when you're there, you will know exactly what you will order and how many WWUs you will be spending, and you will spare yourself the discomfort of making on-the-spot decisions. In other words, you order at home just as if you were shopping from a mail-order catalogue.

Question: Will I still lose weight if I eat breakfast and lunch on Saturday?
Answer: Yes, you will still lose weight. It is very important that you eat three meals each day on The Wild Weekend Diet so that your body will have all the energy it needs to burn off its fat.

Question: I encounter a big problem when we're waiting in the cocktail lounge to be seated at the restaurant. When I join my husband for a few drinks before dinner, there is always some type of snack right in front of me. I find these peanuts and pretzels irresistible. What can I do?
Answer: First of all, make a reservation and arrive just before you are to be seated. Ask your husband if you can have your drink at the dinner table instead of in the lounge. At your table you have three choices. You may order a cocktail and no snack. Or you may have a diet soda free of charge (no WWUs). Or you can ask for some crudités and Perrier water and enjoy that while your husband is enjoying his cocktails and crisps. Of course you may wind up waiting anyway, restaurants not being 100 per cent perfect in honouring reservations. If that happens, know that you gave it your best try. And, all options are still open to you. If you elect to nibble, that's fine, just count your Wild Weekend Units and your diet plan will stay intact. An important thing to remember is that you are not helpless because of the way things have always been in the past. You can change and adopt new thin behaviours. It's up to you!

Question: Whenever I am dieting I find that wine or alcohol hits me very quickly and then I lose control and I begin to pick at everything in sight. Do you have any suggestions?
Answer: This is very common. When you diet, you eat less, and therefore you feel the effects of alcohol more quickly.

To avoid the sudden 'high' try watering down your drink. Ask that the mixers be served on the side so that you can pour in as much as you want at a time. We know of one lady who loves Scotch and soda. She orders one drink with two glasses of soda. That way the measure of Scotch is split between two drinks. You might like a white wine spritzer – it's diluted with soda water. You take longer to finish this tall drink, and your body has time to absorb the alcohol. A very good tip is to eat before you drink; even a salad will help your body to absorb the alcohol more effectively.

Instead of picking at everything in sight, order a prawn cocktail or a salad to eat, or enjoy some cheese and crisp bread. Before you go out, decide what you'll eat with your drink, and stick to your plan.

Question: I have a hard time controlling myself when the bread basket is placed in front of me on the table. Help!
Answer: Again, on The Wild Weekend Diet you don't have to deny yourself the foods you love best. Eat some bread! Just count this bread into your WWUs. You can have your bread and lose weight, too.

Question: There seems to be a tremendous amount of food on the Wild Weekend Saturday night dinners. Do I have to eat it all? Do I have to use all my WWUs?
Answer: No, you do not have to spend your total Wild Weekend allotment. That is your limit, not a 'have-to'. As long as you eat a well-balanced meal that consists of meat, fish or poultry and a salad and vegetable, you do not have to eat any more. In fact, you will be doing your diet a favour by eating fewer WWUs and causing a faster weight loss.

You need never over-eat on The Wild Weekend Diet. The plan was created for those people who want to eat more on the weekend and for whom dieting was an ever-long struggle with temptations, which, in the past, led to failure.

Question: My husband's boss takes us out to dinner very frequently and he insists that we order big, lavish meals. When I am dieting, I am put in a very awkward position as I don't want to offend my husband's boss. Do you have any suggestions?

Answer: Just as big gifts can come in small packages, so, too, can lavish meals come in small calorie counts. To our mind an evening that includes champagne, prawn cocktail, Caesar salad, lobster, asparagus, and fresh fruit is elegant indeed. The bill for this meal is impressive, but the calorie count and, therefore, the WWU value is low.

Question: What do you think of a person who is dieting and orders all kinds of foods from the menu, then only eats half of everything?
Answer: I think that this person is diet-intelligent. This sounds like a person who is serious about losing weight but is intent on not feeling deprived of variety and is willing to put limits on food. Seems like a fun person to have dinner with.

Question: How can I handle a pushy waiter or waitress? It seems as if they are trained to get me to order certain foods when I really don't want them.
Answer: You are very perceptive when you say you think they are trained to behave in such a manner. They are! There are some who are trained how to ask questions in such a way as to receive an order. An example of this is 'What can I bring you from the bar?' rather than 'Would you care for something from the bar?' or 'We have apple, blackberry or cherry pie, which one do you want?' rather than 'Would you like some pie?' They are trained to get you to order. As long as you are aware of their techniques, you can be prepared to answer in a way that suits you and your diet. You can say 'Thank you, I'll have the apple pie' and you can also say 'Thank you, I don't care for any dessert.' Listen to the question, think about whether or not you want dessert, then give the answer you want to give.

Question: I think the most difficult part of eating out is ordering from the menu. Everything is so tempting, and there are always foods I cannot prepare at home. How can I avoid going crazy and ordering everything?
Answer: Menus are designed to trigger your appetite. If this is a problem for you, as it is for many of us, you don't have to open the menu. If you have taken the time as suggested to plan your

meal at home and count your WWUs so that you remain within your total unit count, you can order from your own list. Be prepared with your own made-at-home menu, and you will succeed.

Question: I guess you could call me a martyr. I never eat anything fattening in front of people when I eat out. But the minute I get home, I go on a crazy binge. I want to stop this, but I don't know how.
Answer: Closet eaters are very common; you are not alone in this action. Many overweight people feel very self-conscious about ordering high calorie foods in front of others for fear of hearing a remark such as 'No wonder she's the size she is, look at what she eats.' This is cruel, and it certainly doesn't make you feel terrific.

When you eat lightly in the company of others, you feel deprived because everyone else is eating as they choose. Alone and left out, you may very well go home and comfort yourself with private eating, where no one can see or criticise you. So you see, one of the greatest advantages of The Wild Weekend Diet is that you can eat whatever you want without fear of gaining weight. You won't feel deprived and you won't be deprived, nor will you need to go home and binge. You 'binge' legally, with family or friends. No more Lone Ranger at the Dining Table. Don't be ashamed to tell them you have a special diet Monday to Friday and can enjoy a Wild Weekend.

Question: I am a veteran dieter. I don't ever want to go back to eating butter, sugar, ice cream and mayonnaise again. These foods are part of the reason I gained weight in the first place. Why do you allow them on your diet?
Answer: There is no such thing as a good or bad food for dieting. All foods have been made available on The Wild Weekend Diet. You have the choice of selecting only the foods you want. Other people may want to enjoy butter, sugar or mayonnaise because they are foods they miss most on a diet, but you don't have to eat them. You sound like a very strong and determined dieter. Stick to your guns.

· CHAPTER SIX ·

HOLIDAYS AND SPECIAL OCCASIONS

Holidays

Holidays offer some of us a chance to relax, to take time off from schedules and hassles, a time to lie on the beach or do our own thing.

For others, vacations are viewed as opportunities for adventure, a period in which to travel, see the sights, explore the excitement of modern world cities.

Whichever mode of vacation suits us best, we all share the experience of enjoying a departure from our usual routine. A change. A break. A time away.

All of us who diet must decide how to keep our commitment to weight loss and how to deal with our diet regime during these special and precious days.

Clearly, each of us has a choice. And we need to recognise that we do. We can pack our diet and take it with us, or we can leave it behind with the rest of our routines and schedules.

Then, too, there's a third choice to explore. We can maintain our weight on holiday. This third choice calls for us to practise some control when we're away so that when we come home, we are rewarded by the dial on the scales.

Of course, you can ignore all of the above, but that's the worst choice. After all, it is your body and life, and you are responsible for what happens to you whether you are at home or whether you are on vacation. It's your body, your life and your goals. You owe it to yourself to make up your mind about what you want most.

HOLIDAYS AND SPECIAL OCCASIONS

Here in the real world, holiday eating is one eating-out experience after another. Therefore, all the tips we gave you in the previous chapter on restaurant eating apply to holiday eating as well. Additionally, here are some special holiday tips and experiments for you to try.

- Wherever you go, whatever you do, keep in your mind, at all times, your arrival home and your weighing in. Congratulate yourself on your ability to decide what you want to do.

- Be conscious of your slimming body whether you are sunning on the beach or walking in the cities.

- Take along this book. One very clever and successful dieter said, 'If I can't leave my fat at home, then I can't leave my diet at home, either!'

- Continue to eat a balanced diet and three meals a day. Food nutrition will help you feel your best while you're on holiday.

- Plan your dining in advance. Grilled fish or chicken will always be a better choice for you than fried foods, holiday or no, diet or not.

- When you're especially hungry, indulge yourself with the vegetables that abound in the city/country/town you're in.

- Ask yourself if you really need cream sauces on vegetables, if you must blow all those calories on fattening sauces.

- Always carry a 'Diet Survival Kit' containing packets of diet dressings and sweeteners. Artificial sweetener is especially handy in foreign countries where diet drinks are often not available.

- When you leave your hotel, pack an orange or an apple in your bag to eat as a snack while sunning on the beach or trotting around the town.

- Order your salad dry, and ask for a wedge of lemon to squeeze over it.

- When eating buffet-style, concentrate on prawn and turkey rather than ham and meatballs. Better yet, avoid buffets.
- Rehearse your nonchalant way of saying 'No, thank you.'
- Before you eat anything, ask yourself, 'Do I really want this?'
- Plan your itinerary to leave time to relax over meals. Vacation is a good time to get in touch with what's happening in the mind and in the heart of your spouse or travelling companion.
- Develop the fine art of conversation, especially at dessert time. Notice how thin people pass up dessert, and let them be an inspiration to you.
- Eat slowly.
- Chew thoroughly. Savour the flavour of those holiday meals you're paying hard-earned money for.
- If you feel like it, ask for a Virgin Mary, a Bloody Mary without vodka, or a fresh orange juice.
- At get-togethers, station yourself next to a thin person. Watching the way thin people eat and drink is inspirational and practical.
- Keep thinking thin.
- Plan your itinerary to include plenty of exercise. Don't just loll around the ship or hotel pool; really swim in it every day you're there. Take time out from your busy schedule to play some tennis; don't let your game get rusty.
- Make sure your sight-seeing includes plenty of good, healthy walking. Walk briskly to increase the calorie burn-up.
- Reward yourself for good, diet-conscious behaviour by buying yourself something wonderful and non-calorific.
- Be careful not to get overtired. Fatigue weakens your willpower.
- Avoid booking full-board holidays. Being faced with three

large meals a day is too tempting. If you are half-board you can select an appropriate lunch with great ease.
- You don't have to eat all that you paid for. Give yourself permission to get what you really want from your vacation. Above all, have a good time!

Birthdays and other special occasions

Every day is somebody's something.

Just think about it. If it's not your birthday or anniversary, then it's probably someone else's special occasion, or will be shortly. If you're searching for an excuse to go off your diet, it's not difficult to find one!

We dedicate the following information (ammunition you will need to combat the external excuses) so that you can accomplish your goal. You can succeed in the face of eating agendas – yours and those of everybody else in the munching world.

Ammunition for those Anniversary Occasions

'I made your favourite dessert.'
  'Try just one.'
  'One won't hurt.'
  'You look fine to me.'

Our social whirl is so often an eating world, isn't it? And sometimes other people have a hard time enjoying themselves when they know you're holding back. Whatever the psychological reason for this, the phenomenon is true. And so they try to persuade you from your goals. What you need to remember here is how you'll feel best. And that means the day after as well as at the moment. Here is some ammunition for those inevitable events.

1. You *never* have to eat to please someone else.
2. The Wild Weekend Diet permits you to spend your WWUs in any way you like.
3. Be aware of portion sizes and specific Wild Weekend Unit counts of all foods you eat.

4. Eating *before* you go to someone's home is a standard diet lifesaver, especially before a cocktail or buffet party, then you can keep away from the food.
5. While at the party, pile on the salad, drink plenty of sparkling water, and talk, talk, talk throughout the entire meal!
6. Keep track of your WWUs as you eat them.
7. On some level be aware of your strategies and goals at all times.
8. If you feel you need WWUs every day in order to enjoy your social life, look at Chapter 10, The Core Diet, for a different approach to dieting.

The following are some sample foods that might be offered at parties. Their Wild Weekend Units have been calculated from the base information in Chapters 7, 8 and 9. In other words, the following food values are listed either in those chapters or the recipes have been broken down to yield a Wild Weekend Unit count.

AT HOME/SPECIAL OCCASION WILD WEEKENDS

SATURDAY NIGHT SUPPER PARTY/ BIRTHDAY/ANNIVERSARY

	WWUs
White wine spritzer, 2	2
Cheese Savors, 20 pieces	1
Cocktail sausages with dip	4
Lasagna	8
Salad with fresh lemon	0
Courgettes	0
Chocolate cake, iced	5
Coffee with cream	1
	21

COLD BUFFET PARTY

	WWUs
White wine, 2 glasses	2
Cocktail Savouries, 2	2
Cold meat platter:	
Turkey breast, 2 oz (50 g)	2
Roast Beef, 2 oz (50 g)	4
Salami, ½ oz (12 g)	1
Roll and mustard	2
Pickles, sweet mixed, 1 tablespoon	1
Salad with 2 tablespoons Italian dressing	3
Cheesecake	4
	21

BARBECUE

	WWUs
Beer, light, 24 fl oz (700 ml) (2 cans)	2
Hot dog with bun	4
Hamburger with bun	7
Potato salad, ½ mug	3
Coleslaw, ½ mug	2
Green salad, plain	0
Ice cream	2
	20

CHRISTMAS DINNER

	WWUs
Gin and low calorie tonic, 2 glasses	2
White wine, dry, 2 glasses	2
Grapefruit cocktail	1
Roast turkey, 6 oz (170 g)	4
Bacon roll, 1	1

Stuffing, 3 tablespoons	2
Gravy, homemade, ¼ mug	2
Brussels sprouts	0
Carrots	0
Roast potato, 1 small	1
Bread sauce, 2 tablespoons	1
Cranberry sauce, 2 tablespoons	1
Christmas pudding	3
Brandy butter, 2 tablespoons	3
Coffee, black	0
	23

EASTER SUNDAY

	WWUs
Sherry, medium, 2 glasses	2
Red wine, 2 glasses	2
Roast leg lamb, 6 oz (170 g)	5
New potatoes, 6 oz (170 g)	2
Butter, 2 teaspoons	1
Gravy, ¼ mug homemade	2
Mint sauce	0
Peas	1
Carrots	0
Cauliflower	0
White sauce, thin, ¼ mug	1
Lemon meringue pie, homemade	4
Coffee with cream and sugar	2
	22

The Catered Affair

Weddings and special anniversary parties are some of the happy occasions that take place outside a home environment. As the number of guests can vary from ten to a hundred or more, so, too, can the courses run from four to ten.

Generally, though, the catered affair is easier on the dieters. For starters, host and hostess will be socialising, not pressing food on each and every guest, not chasing you down the hall with the Baked Alaska, so the pressure is off. Also, there is, generally, little opportunity for second helpings.

It's likely, though, that you'll still need to assert yourself from time to time. You know how to do that by now. And, best of all, you have your WWUs to spend, so it should be a wonderful affair. To help you along, here are some hints:

- Don't eat what you don't want to eat.
- Ask for meat and salads without gravies and dressings, if that's the way you'd like to eat them. The WWU choices are still up to you to make.
- Eat only what you planned to eat.
- Stop eating when you feel satisfied.
- When you're finished, make a trip to the cloakroom and brush your teeth and freshen up. With a little luck, your plate will be gone by the time you return.
- Don't eat food you don't like. Make this a diet maxim of yours. In fact, make it a lifetime maxim of yours.
- Call the hotel or caterer. This is easier than speaking directly with the hostess. Tell him or her that you will be a guest at the function and that you would like to know what will be served. Take out your copy of *The Wild Weekend Diet*, get a pencil and a piece of paper and start allotting your WWUs. Knowing exactly what you will eat and the number of WWUs you will spend, you will be going prepared.
- Check over the following menus so that you'll have an idea of what you might be served and what the foods are worth in WWU counts.

SAMPLE MENUS

CATERED RECEPTION (1) WWUs

Whisky, 1	1
Red wine, 2 glasses	2
Cocktail savouries, 2 pieces	2
Sirloin steak, grilled, 6 oz (170 g)	6
Bearnaise sauce, 2 tablespoons	2
Tossed green salad with 2 tablespoons oil and vinegar	3
Mashed potato, ½ mug	2
Eclair, custard-filled, chocolate icing	3
Coffee, black	0
	21

CATERED RECEPTION (2) WWUs

Champagne, 2 glasses	2
Egg mayonnaise	4
Roll with 1 tablespoon butter	3
Gammon, grilled with pineapple, 6 oz (170 g)	7
Potato, baked	2
Green beans	0
Meringue	3
Coffee with cream	1
	22

CATERED RECEPTION (3) WWUs

Sherry, medium, 1 glass	1
Spring water	0

Cream of mushroom soup	2
Roast chicken, 6 oz (170 g)	8
Gravy, ¼ mug, homemade	2
Stuffing, 3 tablespoons	2
Mashed potato, ½ mug	2
Apple pie	4
Coffee, black	0
Brandy, 1	1
	22

Business lunches

Many men and women find these occasions an essential part of their business lives yet ruinous to their diet and health. Meals are invariably chosen to be impressive. All too often that means lavish in quantity and lavish in cream, whether the meals are eaten at restaurants or in directors' dining rooms.

Business entertaining should not be an excuse for giving up your mid-week diet. If you have a quiet weekend ahead you may wish to swop one day's business entertaining for your Saturday's WWUs, but if you want to have fun at the weekend as well then you need to be prepared.

- When you are host or hostess, go to restaurants where you know the menu well, preferably where fish or a cold buffet is served. Ring in advance and check that they can prepare the food and drinks your diet requires.

- When ordering drinks, have your Slimline tonic without gin but with a slice of lemon, your Slimline soda or dry ginger without whisky but on the rocks. Order wine plus a bottle of Perrier water and stick to the latter yourself. Women, in particular, are drinking very little alcohol at business lunches today.

- Asparagus, mange tout and calabrese are all 'free' vegetables, so order these as starters to have with your main course. Always ask for dressings to be served on the side.

- For your main course you are allowed 3 oz (80 g) protein food. You don't have to order a cottage cheese salad every time! Try grilled giant prawns, sole or trout, poached salmon, or roast poussin, pheasant, guinea fowl or venison. But ask for it to be served without sauce.

- If you are expected to have a starter or a dessert, try melon to start, or have a few delicious strawberries, a slice of fresh pineapple or other food from your daily snack allowance to finish.

- Quickly assess your guests before the meal – if they are overweight you will be doing them a favour to take them to a restaurant where they *can* choose low calorie food; if they are thin, that is where they would probably prefer to eat anyway!

- Nouvelle cuisine restaurants may be a good choice, their portions are decoratively appetising, yet small. But remember that those velvety vegetable sauces can mask lashings of cream. Ring and ask which are really low calorie dishes before you book your table.

- If you are eating in a directors' dining room make sure you have a round table discussion – the success of the company depends on the health of its directors. Insist that your Cordon Bleu cook does not kill you all off with kindness. Make sure sauces and dressings are optional, that there are plenty of delicious salads and that vegetables are steamed yet crisp. Ask for good fresh fruit, and not just luscious all-too-tempting puds.

· CHAPTER SEVEN ·

APPETISERS AND ACCOMPANIMENTS

And now to the nitty-gritty of WWU values. This chapter, along with Chapters 8 and 9, lists nearly every food you'll come across on your Wild Weekend, from finger foods to desserts. You'll need to spend time learning how unit values are determined. It's time well spent because when you're through, you'll be able to do an accurate count on anything and everything edible – from the simplest cocktails to elaborate gourmet entrées and heavenly, creamy, gooey, desserts.

Many selections combine two or more ingredients. With simple combinations, The Diet Workshop merely took the calorie count available in numerous calorie-counting books and assigned a unit value per serving based on calories. This method applies to breads, rolls, soups, snacks, salad dressings, vegetables, fruits and beverages.

For more complicated items, we checked basic cookbook recipes, listed all significant ingredients, omitting spices, lemon juice, bouillon and other substances that are practically without calories, and assigned calorie counts to each ingredient. Then we added up the total calories for that recipe. Next we divided the recipe into an average serving size. For the main courses, we worked on calories for a 6 oz (170 g) cooked portion of meat, fish or poultry. Finally we assigned a unit value for that serving.

Simple? Most good ideas are! But that doesn't mean you have licence to assume that the unit values are 100 per cent accurate. Recipes from different sources differ in ingredients and in amounts of ingredients. You can assume that the unit values listed are a good approximation, and remember the Wild Weekend maxim: *You never go wrong when you count high.*

The following information gives you freedom of choice over what you eat and, ultimately, how you look and feel.

APPETISERS AND STARTERS

	WWUs		WWUs
Anchovies, 6	1	kippered fillet	
Ardennes pâté 4 oz		3½ oz (100 g)	3
(115 g) and toast	9	roll mop, 1	3
Artichoke (globe) and		Hors d'oeuvres, mixed	6
1 tablespoon butter	2	Meatballs in barbecue	
Asparagus and		sauce, 2	2
1 tablespoon butter	2	Melon and Parma	
Avocado and prawns	7	ham	3
vinaigrette	6	Melon slice	1
Barbecued spareribs, 3	6	Mortadella, 1 oz	
Bombaymix,		(25 g)	2
1 tablespoon	1	Mussels in wine sauce,	
Canapés, 1	1	6	2
Cannelloni	6	Oysters, 6–8	1
Caviar, 1 tablespoon	1	Potted shrimps and	
Cheese straws, 2	1	bread	5
Chicken liver pâté and		Prawn cocktail	3
toast	5	Prosciutto, 1 oz (25 g)	1
Chopped liver,		Risotto, 7 oz (200 g)	4
2 tablespoons	2	Roll and butter	3
Cocktail sausage rolls,		Salad Niçoise	4
2	1	Salami, 1 oz (25 g)	2
Cocktail sausage with		Scallop Mornay	5
dip, 1	1	Scampi fried, 4 oz	
Corn on the cob, 1		(115 g)	4
tablespoon butter	3	Seviche, 1 serving	2
Egg mayonnaise	4	Smoked eel, 4 oz	
Grapefruit cocktail	1	(115 g)	4
Herring in sauce		Smoked salmon, 2 oz	
3½ oz (100 g)	3	(50 g), buttered bread	3

APPETISERS AND ACCOMPANIMENTS

	WWUs		WWUs
Smoked trout and horseradish	3	Tortellini in cream sauce	7
Smoked trout pâté, 4 oz (115 g) and toast	6	Whitebait, fried, 2 oz (50 g)	4
Spaghetti Bolognaise, 5 oz (140 g)	6	Vol au vent, large cocktail, 1	2
		small cocktail, 1	1
Taramasalata, 4 oz (115 g) and toast	6	starter size	6

DIPS
(1 oz/25 g unless noted)

	WWUs		WWUs
Bacon and horseradish	1	Hummus, 2 tablespoons	2
Blue cheese	1		
Cream cheese	2	Onion	1
Garlic	1	French	1
Green Goddess	1	Tartar	1
Guacamole, ¼ mug	2	Barbecue	1

GRAINS

Grains come in different packages. What they share is that they are cereal seeds. The US Cancer Institute advises that we should choose whole grains (whole seeds) over crushed grains, such as flour, to keep us on the path of most resistance to cancer. For our good health, wholemeal products which are naturally high in fibre are always preferable to highly refined white.

You'll find the grain category broken down into various subcategories that will make it easy for you to look up the foods you are searching for when you want to know their unit values. The categories that follow are Breads, Cereals, Crackers, Rolls and Miscellaneous Grains.

BREADS
(1 oz/25 g unless noted)

	WWUs
Banana nut	2
Banana tea	2
Bran raisin	2
Breadsticks, 2	1
Brown	1
Coburg	1
Cracked wheat	1
Currant loaf	1
Date nut	2
French	1
Fried bread	3
Fruit malt loaf	1
Garlic bread	2
Gingerbread	2
Granary	1
Hovis	1
Malt loaf	1
Pitta bread, small round	1
white or wholewheat, oval	2
Pumpernickel	1
Raisin	1
Rye	1
Slimcea, 2	1
Soda bread	1
Soft sandwich	1
Toasted bread	2
Vienna	1
VitBe	1
Walnut loaf	2
Wheat germ	1
White bread, large loaf	1
thin slice, 1	1
medium/thick slice, 1	2
small loaf	1
Wholemeal, large loaf, medium/thick slice, 1	2
small loaf slice, 1	1
Wholewheat	1

CEREALS
(1 mug unless noted)

	WWUs
All-Bran, Kellogg's	2
Alpen	3
Bemax, 1 oz (25 g)	2
Bran, 100%	2
Bran Buds	2
Bran Flakes	2
Breakfast biscuit, 1	2
Cocoa Krispies	2
Corn Flakes	2
Corn Flakes, sugar coated 1 oz (25 g)	2
Country Bran	2
Country Store, Jordans	2
Crunchy Nut Flakes	2
Frosted Rice, Kellogg's 1 oz (25 g)	2
Frosties, 1 oz (25 g)	2
Fruit 'n' Fibre	2
Granola, 1 oz (25 g)	2
Grape Nuts, 1 oz (25 g)	2
Harvest Crunch, 1 oz (25 g)	2
Honey & Almond Crunch, Jordans, 1 oz (25 g)	2
Honey Snacks	2
Muesli, ½ mug	2
Oat Flakes	2

APPETISERS AND ACCOMPANIMENTS

	WWUs
Oatmeal, 1 oz (25 g)	2
Original Crunchy cereal, 1 oz (25 g)	2
Porridge (cooked)	2
Porridge oats, 1 oz (25 g)	2
Puffa Puffa Rice, Kellogg's	2
Puffed Oats, plain or sweetened, 1 oz (25 g)	2
Puffed Rice, 2 mugs	2
Puffed Wheat, 2 mugs	2
Raisin Bran, Kellogg's	2
Ready Brek, 1 oz (25 g) dry	2
Rice Krispies	2
Rice Toasties	2
Ricicles	2
Shredded Wheat, 1 biscuit	2
spoon size	3
Shreddies	3
Smacks	2
Special K	2
Start	3
Sugar Puffs	2
Swiss style cereal	2
Toasted Farmhouse bran, 1 oz (25 g)	2
Weetabix, 1	2
Weetabix Farmhouse harvest nuts, 1 oz (25 g)	2
Weetaflakes	2
Weetaflakes 'n' Raisins	2
Wheatgerm, 2 tablespoons	1

CRACKERS

	WWUs
Bath Olivers, 1	1
Cheese Extra Specials, 1	1
Cheeselets, 18	1
Cheese Sandwich Biscuit, 1	1
Cheese Savors, 20	1
Cheese Snaps, 16	1
Cheese Thins, 3	1
Cracker Bread, 2	1
Cream crackers, 2	1
Cream puffs, 1	1
Digestives, 1	1
Dutch Crispbread, 2	1
Hovis Crackers, 2	1
Kracka Wheat, 2	1
Macvita, 1	1
new, 2	1
Melba rounds, 5	1
Oatcakes, 2 small	1
Potato crisps, 16	2
Ritz Cheese, Nabisco, 6	1
Rusk, 1	1
Rye bran crispbreads, 3	1
extra thin, 6	1
Rye crispbreads, 2	1
extra thin, 3	1
Ryking crispbread, 2	1
Ryvita, 2	1
Tuc, 2	1
Vita Wheat/Rye, 3	1
Water biscuits, 2	1
Wheat biscuit thins, 3	1
Wheaten crackers, 2	1
Wholemeal bran biscuits, 1	1
crispbreads, 2	1
Zwieback, 2	1

ROLLS
(1, unless noted)

	WWUs
Bagel	3
Bap	2
Bridge roll, large	2
small	1
Cloverleaf roll	2
Croissant	4
small	3
Crumpet	2
Crusty roll	2
Currant bun	2
Dinner roll	1
Frankfurter or hot dog roll	2
Hamburger roll	2
Hotcross bun	2
Iced bun	3
Muffin	2
Poppy seed roll	2
Scone	2
Toasted teacake	2
Waffle, small round	1
oblong	2
Wholemeal roll	2

MISCELLANEOUS GRAINS

	WWUs
Arrowroot, 2 tablespoons	1
Barley, pearl, 1 oz (25 g)	2
Breadcrumbs, 1 oz (25 g)	1
Cornflour, 2 tablespoons	1
Corn fritter 2" × 1½" (5 cm × 4 cm)	2
Cornmeal, cooked, 1 mug	2
yellow, dry, 1 mug	7
Digestive crumbs, ½ mug	6
Flour, buckwheat, 1 mug	4
carob, 1 oz (25 g)	1
potato, 1 oz (25 g)	2
rice, ½ mug	3
wheat, unsifted, ½ mug	3
wholemeal, 1 oz (25 g)	2
Macaroni dry, 4 oz (115 g)	6
1 tablespoon	1
Matzo meal, ½ mug	3
Pancake, 7" (18 cm) diameter, 1	2
French crêpe, 7" (18 cm)	1
Scotch, 1, 2½" (7 cm) diameter	1
Pasta, dry, all types, 2 oz (50 g)	3
Rice, dry, all types, 2 oz (50 g)	3
Sago, dry, 1 tablespoon	1
Semolina, dry, 2 tablespoons	1
Spaghetti, dry, 4 oz (115 g)	6
Tabouli (bulgar wheat), 1 oz (25 g)	2
Tacos, 2 shells, 6" (16 cm) diameter	2
Tapioca, dry, 2 tablespoons	1
Tortilla, corn, fried, 1 average	2

APPETISERS AND ACCOMPANIMENTS

SOUPS
(1 mug unless noted)

	WWUs		WWUs
Asparagus, Cream of,		Chicken stock,	
made with milk	3	homemade	1
Cream of, tinned	2	Game soup	2
Beans with Pork, made		Leek, Cream of, made	
with water	2	with milk	3
Beef and Vegetable,		Lentil	4
condensed and		Main Course soups	3
diluted	1	Minestrone	2
Beef Broth	2	homemade	3
Beef, Chunky	3	Sainsbury's, with	
Beef cube, ½	0	croûtons	2
Beef flavoured,		Mulligatawny,	
Cup-a-Soup, 1		homemade	2
packet	1	Mushroom, Cream of,	
Beef noodle,		homemade	3
Cup-a-Soup, 1		Cream of, tinned or	
packet	1	dried	2
Beef stock	1	Onion	2
Borscht	2	French, with 1 slice	
Celery, Cream of	2	bread topped with	
Chicken and Celery,		2 oz (50 g) cheese	5
low calorie	1	Oxtail	2
Chicken and Noodle,		Cup-a-Soup, 1	
condensed and		packet	1
diluted	2	low calorie	1
dried	1	with vegetables	2
Chicken and		Pea, Cup-a-Soup, 1	
Vegetable	2	packet	2
Chicken Broth	2	Main course	3
Chicken, Cream of	2	Split	2
Cream of,		Split with ham	2
Campbell's	3	Salmon Bisque	3
Cup-a-Soup	2	Spring Vegetable,	
Chicken soup	2	condensed, diluted	1
low calorie	1	dried	1
Chicken stock, cube, ½	0	tinned	2

	WWUs		WWUs
Tomato,		Vegetable and Noodle	1
made with milk	2	Vegetable,	
made with water	2	Sainsbury's	1
tinned or dried	2	Scotch	1
Tomato and Bacon	2	tinned and dried	2
Tomato and Beef	2	vegetarian	2
Tomato and		Venison	2
Vegetable	2	Vichyssoise,	
Vegetable and Beef		homemade	3
Broth	2	tinned	2
Vegetable and Lentil	2		

SNACKS

In the Snack category you will find sweets and chocolate, crunchies and nuts.

SWEETS AND CHOCOLATE *(1 oz/25 g unless noted)*	WWUs		WWUs
		Brazil nut toffee, 2	1
		Butterscotch	2
		Caramel, chocolate	
Aero, medium, 1	3	chocolate flavoured	
large, 1	6	roll	2
After Eights, 3	1	chocolate with nuts	2
Almonds, sugared	2	Cherry, chocolate	
Bar 6, 1	3	covered, 2 pieces	2
Boiled sweets, 3	1	Chewing gum, 1 piece	0
Bonbons, 2	1	8 pieces	1
Bounty, fun size	2	Chocolate bar, 100 g	7
single	2	bittersweet	2
Bournville Chocolate		milk chocolate	2
bar, 100 g	6	mint chocolate	2
Bournville Chocolate		semisweet	2
and Roasted		Chocolate buttons,	
Almond, 100 g	7	small bag	4
Bournville Fruit &		Chocolate coated	
Nut, 100 g bar	6	fudge	2

APPETISERS AND ACCOMPANIMENTS

	WWUs		WWUs
with caramel and peanuts	2	Liquorice pastilles	2
with nuts	2	Liquorice toffee, 1	1
Chocolate Eclair, 2 sweets	1	Liquorice twist, 2 pieces	1
Chocolate Flake	2	Lockets, 1 packet	2
Chocolate peppermint creams	2	Lollies, small, 1	1
		Lozenges, 4	1
Chocolate coated peanuts	2	Maltesers, 7	1
Chocolate coated raisins	2	Marathon, fun size	2
		single	3
Chocolate rum truffles	2	Mars Bar, fun size	2
Chocolate toffees, 2	1	single	5
Coconut Bar	2	Marshmallows, 4 large	2
Coconut Neapolitan	2	Matchmakers, 9	1
Coolmints, 12	1	long, 3	1
Dolly Mixture	2	Milk Tray Assortment	2
Double Decker	2	Milky Way, fun size	1
Extra Strong Mints, 7	1	single	2
Fruit & nut dessert bar, 1	4	Mints, butter, 6	1
		Mints, chocolate covered	2
Fruit Gums, 1 tube	1	Mint crisps	2
Fruit pastilles, 1 tube	2	Mint humbugs	2
Fry's Chocolate Cream, 100 g bar	6	Mints or peppermints, after dinner, all kinds	2
Fudge, 1 cubic inch	2	Murraymints, 3	1
Fudge Bar	2	Opal Fruits, 4	1
Glacier Mints, 6	1	Orange slices	2
Hundreds and Thousands, 1 tablespoon	1	Peanut bars	2
		Peanut brittle	2
		Polo, 1 tube	2
Jelly babies	2	Pontefract Cakes	2
small bag	3	Popcorn	2
Jelly beans	2	Popcorn caramel, ¾ oz (20 g)	3
Kendal Mint Cake	2		
KitKat, 2 bar	2	Refreshers, 12	1
4 bar	4	Revels, per pack	3
Lion bar, 1	3	Rollo, per pack	4
Liquorice Allsorts, 2	1	Sherbet lemons, 3	1

	WWUs
Sherbet powder	2
Smarties, 1 tube	3
Tic Tacs, 15	1
Toffee, all flavours, 2 pieces	1
Toffo, per pack	5
Topic bar	4
Trebor Mints, 9	1
Treets, per pack	4
Turkish Delight	2
Twix, per pack	2
Walnut Whip, 1	3
Yorkie Bar,	
chocolate, 1	5
nut, 1	5
raisin, 1	4

SAVOURY CRUNCHIES
(1 oz/25 g unless noted)

	WWUs
Cheese Puffs	2
Cheese Savors, 20	1
Cheese Savouries, 5	1
Cheese Snaps, 20	1
Cheese Sticks	2
Chipples	2
Corn shapes, all flavours	2
Popcorn, air popped, 3 mugs	1
Potato crisps, all brands	2
Potato sticks	2
Pork scratchings	2
Pretzels, 3 rings	2
Twiglets	1

NUTS

	WWUs
Almond paste, 1 oz (25 g)	2
Almonds, in shell, 12	1
roasted, 1 oz (25 g)	2
shelled, chopped, 1 tablespoon	1
slivered, 1 oz (25 g)	2
Brazil nuts, 4–5 large	2
shelled, ⅓ mug	8
Cashews, roasted, 6–8	2
roasted, 1 mug	8
Chestnuts, 10	2
fresh, scant ½ mug	3
Coconut desiccated, 1 oz (25 g)	3
fresh, 1″ × 1″ (2.5 × 2.5 cm) piece	1
fresh, shredded, 1 oz (25 g)	2
Hazelnuts, 10–12	2
Macadamia nuts, roasted, 6 whole	2
Mixed nuts, shelled, 8–12	2
Peanuts, chopped, 1 tablespoon	1
dry roast, 25	1
raw, 1 oz (25 g)	2
roasted, 1 tablespoon	2
Pecans, chopped, 1 tablespoon	1
large, 10	3
Pine nuts, shelled, 1 oz (25 g)	2
Pistachio nuts, unshelled, 30	2

	WWUs		WWUs
Pumpkin seeds, dry, hulled 1 oz (25 g)	2	Sunflower seeds, shelled, ½ oz (12 g)	1
Safflower seed kernels, 1 oz (25 g)	3	Tiger nuts, 1 oz (25 g)	2
Sesame seeds, dry, hulled, 1 tablespoon	1	Walnuts, 8–15 halves black, 8–10 halves	2
Soybeans, 1 oz (25 g)	1	pickled	2
		chopped, 1 oz (25 g)	2

JAMS, JELLIES, SUGAR, SYRUPS

(1 tablespoon unless noted)

	WWUs		WWUs
Apple and pear spread	1	Lemon Curd	2
Brandy butter	2	Malt, dry, 1 oz (25 g)	2
Candied peel, 1 oz (25 g)	2	Malted milk, dry powder	2
Chocolate, cooking, 1 oz (25 g)	2	Marmalade, all varieties	1
Chocolate spread	1	Marron glacé	2
Cocoa mix, 1 oz (25 g)	2	Mincemeat	1
Cocoa, plain, 2 tablespoons	1	Molasses, cane, Barbados or blackstrap	1
Fish paste	1	Preserves, all varieties	1
Gelatin, unflavoured, 1 packet	0	Sugar, brown	1
Ginger, crystallised, 1 oz (25 g)	2	icing	1
Golden syrup	2	white, 4 cubes	1
Hazelnut & chocolate spread	1	white, granulated/ castor	1
Honey	1	Syrup, chocolate, fudge	1
Jam, all varieties	1	chocolate, low calorie, 5 tablespoons	1
low-calorie, all varieties, 2 tablespoons	1	chocolate, thin type	1
Jelly jam, all varieties	1	maple	1
low calorie, all varieties, 2 tablespoons	1	sorghum	1
		Toppings, 1 oz (25 g)	2

	WWUs		WWUs
Ice Magic	2	3 tablespoons	1
whipped, non-dairy,		Treacle	1

DRESSINGS, OILS AND FATS, AND SALADS

SALADS
(½ mug unless noted)

	WWUs		WWUs
American salad	2	Potato salad with mayonnaise	3
Apple, celery and walnut salad, dressed	3	with salad dressing	2
		St Michael's brand salads	3–4
Cabbage salad, plain no dressing	0	Sea food salad	2
Chef's salad, 1 oz (25 g) each, turkey, ham and cheese, plain	4	Spinach and bacon salad	2
		Tabouli, 1 oz (25 g)	2
		Tomato salad, jellied	1
		Tuna salad	2
Chicken salad	2	Waldorf salad, 1 oz	2
Chicken with celery salad	3	Vegetable salad	2
Coleslaw, diet	1		

DRESSINGS
(1 tablespoon unless noted)

	WWUs
with commercial French dressing	2
with homemade French dressing	2	Bleu/Roquefort	2
with mayonnaise	2	low calorie	1
		Caesar	1
with mayonnaise-type salad dressing	1	low calorie	1
		Coleslaw	1
Crab salad	2	low calorie	1
Egg mayonnaise	4	French	1
Greek salad, 2 oz (50 g) feta cheese, plain	3	homemade	2
		low calorie	1
		Garlic	1
Green salad, plain	0	Green Goddess	1
Ham salad, 1 oz (25 g)	1	low calorie	1
Macaroni salad	2	Herb and garlic	2

APPETISERS AND ACCOMPANIMENTS

	WWUs
Italian	2
low calorie	1
Mayonnaise	2
Miracle Whip, Kraft	2
Oil and vinegar	2
Prawn cocktail sauce	2
Salad cream	1
low calorie	1
Salad dressing, mayonnaise or sour cream type	2
Sweet and sour, Kraft	1
Thousand Island	2
low calorie	1
Vinaigrette	1
Waistline, low calorie, 3 tablespoons	1

OILS AND FATS
(2 teaspoons unless noted)

	WWUs
Bacon fat	1
Butter	2
Chicken fat	1
Cream substitutes, Coffee-mate, 2 tablespoons	1
Lard	1
Margarine	1
low calorie, 1 tbs	1
whipped, 1 tbs	1
Olive oil	1
Salad oil	1
Spry	1
Suet	1
Vegetable oil	1
Vegetable shortening	1

SAUCES AND GRAVIES
(½ mug unless noted)

	WWUs		WWUs
Bearnaise	5	with meat (Bolognese)	2
Bread sauce, 2 tablespoons	1	with meatballs	3
Cheese sauce	4	with mushrooms	2
Cook-in-sauce	3	Marinara sauce	2
Curry sauce	3	Mornay sauce, packet	2
Gravy, homemade	4	Mushroom sauce	2
homemade, light	3	Onion gravy, prepared, mix	1
prepared mix	1	Sauce mix	2
tinned	2	Sour cream sauce	4
Hard sauce (brandy butter)	7	Spanish sauce	2
Hollandaise sauce, mock	5	White sauce, medium	3
		thick	3
Italian sauce (tomato)	2	thin	2

CONDIMENTS, RELISHES, SAVOURY SPREADS, STUFFINGS
(1 tablespoon unless noted)

	WWUs		WWUs
Anchovy sauce, 3 tablespoons	1	Peppers, chilli, pickled, hot, mild, sweet	0
Apple sauce, 3 tablespoons	1	Piccalilli mustard	0
A-1 sauce, 3 tablespoons	1	sweet, 3 tablespoons	1
Barbecue sauce, 3 tablespoons	1	traditional	0
Capers	0	Pickled beetroot	0
Cranberry sauce, 2 tablespoons	1	Pickled cabbage	0
Chilli sauce, 3 tablespoons	1	Pickled cucumber, sweet, 1 large	2
Chutney, 2 tablespoons	1	dill, 1 large	0
Daddies, 3 tablespoons	1	sour, 1 large	0
Dumplings, 1	2	Pickle, sweet, 2 tablespoons	1
Fish paste	1	Pickles, all varieties	1
Horseradish cream	1	Pickled gherkins	0
Horseradish, prepared	0	Pimientos	0
Ketchup, 3 tablespoons	1	Pickled walnuts, 2 tablespoons	1
Marmite, 2 teaspoons	0	Relish, barbecue, 2 tablespoons	1
Meat pastes	1	corn, 3 tablespoons	1
Mint jelly	1	hamburger, 2 tablespoons	1
Mint sauce	0	Soy sauce	0
Mushroom ketchup	0	Sweet and sour sauce, 1 oz (25 g)	1
Mustard	0	Stuffing, homemade, 3 tablespoons	2
Olives, large, black, 5	2	packet, 3 tablespoons	1
green, 10	2	Tabasco sauce	0
Onions, cocktail	0	Tartar sauce	2
pickled	0	Teriyaki sauce, 2 oz (50 g)	1
Oyster sauce	0		

APPETISERS AND ACCOMPANIMENTS

	WWUs		WWUs
Tomato paste, ½ mug	2	Yeast, dry or Brewer's,	
Tomato sauce, ½ mug	1	1 oz (25 g)	2
Vinegar, plain	0	Yorkshire pudding,	
wine or flavoured	0	medium portion	2
Worcestershire sauce	0		

· CHAPTER EIGHT ·

MAIN COURSES, VEGETABLES AND FRUITS

Let's take a minute to discuss main courses and their WWU values. There are main courses . . . and then there are *main courses*: plain grilled chicken or steak and kidney pie! As the range of choices is very large, so are the WWU values. And remember – where you eat the particular dish is important. There is usually a calorie difference between what you eat at home and what you eat out. Foods cost more in calories when they're served to you!

At home you can work out the WWUs just as we have done in this book. List all the ingredients for the particular dish, check the calories from a calorie book, or use the food lists in this book. Each Wild Weekend Unit contains about 75 calories. Total the calories, divide by the number of servings, and assign a WWU value to each serving. A recipe totalling 1,600 calories, which serves 4, gives a 400-calorie serving which converts to 5 WWUs for each person per portion.

At the restaurant, alas, it's usually another story. Here you must depend upon all your senses. Take a hard look. Is it 6 oz (170 g) of cooked meat, fish, or poultry, or is it more? How much butter or oil is on or in it? If you even *suspect* that this food is more fattening than home-cooked, you're probably right. So add more WWUs.

Without putting each ounce of meat into a calorimeter, thereby burning it up and making it unfit to eat, it is virtually impossible to know its caloric value. This is because the amount of fat in the meat, which may not be visible to your eye, can cause a wide swing in the number of calories. Standard sources of caloric values differ from one another. The caloric values of the foods that follow are an approximation based on information from standard sources. The 6 oz (170 g) refers to the size of a portion in the case of a made-up dish, and not the weight of the meat.

MAIN COURSES

FISH
(6 oz/170 g cooked, unless noted)

	WWUs
Anchovy fillets	1
Bass	5
Bloater	6
Caviar, 2 tablespoons	1
Clams, tinned, chopped, drained	2
Cockles, 4 oz (115 g)	1
Cod	2
breaded, small portion	2
dried, salted	3
in batter	7
in batter, small portion	4
in butter sauce	3
steak, fried	3
Crab, fresh, all kinds	2
dressed	3
tinned	3
Eel, raw	5
smoked	7
Fish cakes, 2 oz (50 g)	
fried	2
2 oz (50 g) grilled	1
medium, fried	3
medium, grilled	2

	WWUs
Fish fingers, 1	1
king size, 1	2
Fish loaf, homemade	3
Fish sticks, frozen, 10	5
Flounder	2
Haddock, breaded	4
fried, small portion	2
grilled	3
smoked	3
Hake, raw, 6 oz (170 g)	2
Halibut, raw, 6 oz (170 g)	3
Herring roe, fried	6
roll mop	5
tinned, in tomato sauce	3
Kedgeree	4
Kippers	4
Lobster	2
Lox, ¾ oz (20 g)	1
Mackerel	3
smoked	5
tinned, 4 oz (115 g)	3
Mullet, fried	5
Mussels, 3 oz (80 g)	1
Octopus, raw, 6 oz (170 g)	2

	WWUs		WWUs
Oysters, fried, 4 oz (115 g)	4	Whiting, baked, breaded	4
medium, 6–10	2	fried	5
smoked, Japanese baby, tinned, 3½ oz (100 g)	3	**BEEF** *(6 oz/170 g cooked, unless noted)*	
Plaice fillets	2		WWUs
(frozen) fried in batter	7	Beef bourguignonne	8
(frozen) fried in crumbs	6	Beef croquettes, each	2
Pollack, creamed	3	Beef, frozen (Lean Cuisine)	3
raw, 6 oz (170 g)	2	Beef in barbecue sauce, frozen, 6 oz (170 g)	3
Prawns, 2 oz (50 g)	2		
Prawn salad, 3 oz (80 g)	2	Beefburger, 2 oz (50 g)	2
Roe	4	4 oz (115 g)	4
Salmon, smoked	4	Beef Pot Casserole, 1 pot	3
steak	4	Beef sausages, 1	3
tinned	4	chipolata, 1	2
Sardines, tinned, drained	4	Beef Stroganoff	8
Scallops	3	Braising steak, lean	4
Scampi, 3 oz (80 g)	2	Brisket, braised	9
crumbed, fried, 3 oz (80 g)	4	Corned beef, medium fat	10
Smelt, 4–5 medium	2	tinned	5
Sole	2	Cornish pasties, large	10
Sprats, fried	10	small, 3 oz (80 g)	4
Squid, raw, 6 oz (175 g)	2	Fillet steak	6
Sturgeon, smoked	3	Fore rib roast, lean	6
Trout, brown, raw, whole, 6 oz (170 g)	2	lean and fat	8
rainbow, raw, 6 oz (175 g)	2	Frankfurter, all beef, 4 small	7
Tuna, tinned in brine, 6 oz (170 g)	3	Frozen beef dinner, 11 oz (325 g)	5
in oil, 6 oz (170 g)	4	Goulash, tinned, 4 oz (115 g)	2
Whitebait, fried	12	Hamburger	4
		Meatballs, homemade	6

MAIN COURSES, VEGETABLES AND FRUITS

	WWUs		WWUs
Meat loaf	4	Topside roast, lean	4
Mince fatty (bargain price)	10	lean, 2 slices, 4 oz (115 g)	3
lean	6		
standard	8		

VEAL
(6 oz/170 g cooked unless noted)

	WWUs
Porterhouse steak, lean	5
Pot roast	7
Rib roast	10
Rump steak, grilled, lean	4
lean and fat	5
Salted silverside, lean	4
lean and fat	6
Shepherd's pie (made with 6 oz/170 g meat)	13
8 oz (225 g) portion	5
frozen Birds Eye	4
Sirloin, lean	5
lean and fat	7
Steak teriyaki	12
Steak and kidney pie, individual pastry top or portion, 4 oz (115 g)	5
Steak and kidney pudding, homemade	8
commercial, 4 oz (115 g)	4
Steak and kidney stew	4
Steak pie, pastry top and bottom	7
tinned, 7½ oz (200 g)	4
Stew, homemade, 1 mug	3
Stewing steak	5
T-Bone steak	6

	WWUs
Breast, stewed	8
Chop boned	6
Cordon bleu, 5 oz (140 g)	5
Escalope, breaded (schnitzel)	7
lean only	7
Loin, medium fat	5
Shoulder (blade), lean and roast	5

LAMB
(6 oz/170 g cooked unless noted)

	WWUs
Breast roast	7
Chump chop	5
lean only, 1 average size	2
Cutlets, grilled	6
Irish stew, 1 mug	8
Lancashire hot pot, 1 mug	6
Leg, roast	5
1 slice, 2 oz (50 g)	2
Loin chop	6
Moussaka (frozen)	5
Noisette of lamb	6
Scrag end neck	7
Shoulder, roast	7
1 slice, 2 oz (50 g)	3

PORK
(6 oz/170 g cooked unless noted)

	WWUs
Bacon, Canadian,	
¾ oz (20 g)	1
1 rasher, grilled	1
Gammon boiled leg	4
Danish D shaped	5
rasher lean grilled	4
smoked sliced	6
steak grilled	4
Ham, cured	6
fresh	8
Loin chop	8
Loin roast, lean only	6
Picnic, cured, tinned	7
Pork pie, individual,	
4 oz (115 g)	7
mini, 2 oz (50 g)	3
party, 2½ oz (70 g)	4
slice, 4 oz (115 g)	6
Prosciutto 3 oz (90 g)	3
Sausages	
black pudding	7
cervelat	11
chipolatas, 16 per	
lb (450 g), 1	2
24 per lb (450 g), 1	1
frankfurter, 4	
(6½ oz/180 g)	7
liversausage, coarse	8
liversausage,	
smooth	10
mortadella	8
pepperoni	11
pork and beef	
(450 g)	9
pork, 8 per lb	
(450 g), 1	3
pork, 12 per lb	
(450 g), 1	2
salami	12
Saveloy	6
Vienna, link	10
Sausage rolls	7
mini, 1	2
puff pastry, 1	10
Shoulder (blade)	7
spareribs	7

POULTRY AND GAME
(6 oz/170 g cooked unless noted)

	WWUs
Capon with skin	7
Chicken and vegetable	
pie, 4 oz (115 g)	4
individual	5
Chicken and vegetables	
(Lean Cuisine)	4
Chicken, battered	
crisp, thigh and	
drumstick (with	
bone)	6
Chicken cordon bleu	15
Chicken, dark and	
light, skinless	4
skinless, fried	6
with skin	6
with skin, fried	13
Chicken fricassée,	
homemade, 1 mug	5
Chicken in the basket	9
Chicken Kiev	8
Chicken pie,	
individual	6
Chicken pot casserole	3
Chicken southern	
fried, with bone	6
Chicken stew, tinned,	
1 mug	2

MAIN COURSES, VEGETABLES AND FRUITS

	WWUs		WWUs
Chicken stuffed breasts/thighs	5	chicken, simmered	4
Chicken suprême	4	lamb, fried	5
Chicken tinned, boned	4	ox, stewed	5
Duck, with skin	7	pig, stewed	5
skinless	4	turkey, simmered	4
Goose, with skin	10	Liver and onions, 1 restaurant serving, pan-fried	3
skinless	5		
Hare, raw	3	Sweetbreads	
Pheasant, skinless	4	beef	7
Pigeon, with skin	8	calf	4
skinless	4	lamb, braised	4
Quail, with skin	5	Tongue	
Rabbit, domestic,		calf, braised	4
baked	4	lamb, braised	5
wild, raw	3	ox, braised	5
Turkey escalope, in breadcrumbs	6	Tripe	3
Turkey, light and dark, skinless	4	**LUNCH TREATS** *(3 oz/80 g unless noted)*	
Turkey pie	8		WWUs
Turkey, tinned	4		
Venison, roast	3	Baconburgers	3
		Bacon, 1 rasher, grilled	1
OFFAL *(6 oz/170 g boiled unless noted)*		Bacon, cheese and egg pie	4
	WWUs	Bacon puffs	4
Black pudding	7	Baked Beans and Frankfurters, small tin	4
Brains, all kinds, raw	3		
Chitterlings	8		
Faggots, 1	2	Baked Beans and Hamburger, small tin	4
Haggis, boiled	7		
Heart, beef or lamb braised	4	Baked Beans and Sausages, small tin	5
Kidneys, beef	5	Cheese and onion pastie	4
lamb	3		
veal, raw	3	Crispy pancakes, frozen, stuffed, 1	1
Liver			
calf, fried	6		

	WWUs		WWUs
Ham, boiled	3	Pot Noodles, 1 pot	4
Liver sausage	4	Pot Rice, 1 pot	3
Liverwurst	5	Proscuitto	3
Meat loaf	2	Salami	6
Pâté, country style	4	Spam	3
Pot Casserole, 1 pot	3	Turkey roll	2

EGGS

	WWUs		WWUs
Eggs Benedict, portion	7	yolk, large	1
Duck egg	2	Quail egg	1
Goose egg	2	Quiche Lorraine, homemade, ¼ 7" (18 cm)	5
Hen's egg			
boiled, hard or soft, whole, medium	2	vegetable, homemade, ¼ 7" (18 cm)	3
omelette, plain, 1 egg	2	Scotch eggs, each	3
omelette, Spanish, 1 egg	4	Snack/picnic eggs, each	2
scrambled, 1 egg	2	Turkey egg	2
whites, large, 3	1		

VEGETABLE PROTEINS

(6 oz/170 g unless noted)

	WWUs		WWUs
Bean curd (tofu), firm	3	Peanutbutter, 1 tablespoon	2
soft	2		
Chick peas, ¼ mug	3	Soybeans, dry, cooked ½ mug	2
Lentils, cooked, drained, ½ mug	2	raw, ½ mug	5

PASTA

WWU values for pasta differ depending on whether the dish is homemade, tinned, or restaurant prepared.

For homemade pasta, work out the calories in the same way as you would for any other dish according to the information at the start of this chapter.

The tinned pasta WWU values are consistently low in oil and so low in calories. Measure carefully your correct portion. If you're eating pasta at home, you control the portion size. Count each mug of pasta as 2 WWUs. Add WWUs for the tomato sauce, cheese and any meat in the dish.

In the restaurant, use your eyes. How much pasta is on your plate? A mug? Two mugs? A saucepanful? Allot 2 WWUs for each mug. Check the cheese and sauce. Is it a mug, a ½ mug, or the entire tomato garden? Is it tossed in butter or oil? The WWUs below are based on a 7 oz (200 g) average portion serving unless otherwise noted.

	WWUs		WWUs
Cannelloni, frozen	3	Ravioli, beef, cooked, no sauce	7
Capelletti, cooked, no sauce	7	cheese, cooked, no sauce	7
Fettuccine with cheese	5	in sauce, tinned	3
Lasagna, frozen	4	Spaghetti and meatballs in tomato sauce, 1 mug, tinned	4
homemade	8		
Macaroni cheese, baked, homemade	5		
tinned	3	bolognese sauce, (2 mugs)	12
Pasta shapes, cooked, 1 mug	2	in tomato sauce, tinned (1 mug)	3
uncooked, 3 oz (90 g)	4	Spaghetti, uncooked, 3 oz (90 g)	4
Pasta (2 mugs) with pesto sauce	12	Tortelloni, cooked, no sauce	7
Pot Noodles, 1 packet	4		

FAST FOODS
(regular restaurant serving unless noted)

	WWUs		WWUs
Big Mac, McDonald's	7	Fish and Chips	14
Cheeseburger with bun	4	Hamburger, 8 oz (225 g)	11
Hot dog with bun	4	4 oz (115 g), with bun	7
with cheese and bun	5	with cheese and bun	8
deluxe with cheese and bun	8		

Fast food addendum: A positive aspect of all fast-food restaurants is that the portion sizes are uniform. A McDonald's at Land's End is the same as a McDonald's in London or Blackpool. This consistency of size and calories applies to the items served in most other franchised fast-food restaurants as well.

FOREIGN CUISINES

CHINESE

Chinese food comes in small, regular, large, and you-must-be-kidding portion sizes. Use your eyes to judge, then gauge WWUs accordingly.

Frozen Chinese meals are often marked with calorie content and are lower in fat (WWUs) than authentic Chinese meals. The WWUs below are based on an average-size portion.

	WWUs		WWUs
Chicken chow mein	7	Chop suey with beef, frozen	3
Chicken, fried with chestnuts	7	Duck with bamboo shoots	10
Chicken with mange tout or mushrooms	5	Egg foo yung, 1, with gravy sauce	3
Chicken with peanuts or cashews	6	Egg fried rice	3
		Fried king prawns, 5	4

MAIN COURSES, VEGETABLES AND FRUITS

	WWUs		WWUs
Pancake spring rolls, crispy fried, each	2	Special fried rice	3
Pork with broccoli	4	Stir-fried bean curd and vegetables	2
Prawn crackers, 4	1	Stir-fried chicken	5
Spare ribs, deep fried	12	Stir-fried scallops	2
Spicy pork with bean curd	4	Sweet and sour pork	5
		Sweet and sour prawns	4

FRENCH

The French are famous for their marvellous butter and cream sauces. Our WWUs are figured on an average preparation and serving size. If you detect a lot of butter, add at least 3 WWUs. Use your senses!

	WWUs		WWUs
Auvergne leg of lamb	9	Poulet Basque	10
Beef bourguignonne	8	Quenelles de brochet (Pike quenelles)	7
Beef Wellington	20		
Bouillabaisse	6	Quiche aux champignons (mushroom quiche)	7
Braised rabbit	7		
Coq au vin	11		
Côtes de veau au calvados (veal chops with apple, brandy and cream)	19	Salmon en croûte with sauce	17
		Sole Meunière	4
		Stuffed pheasant	8
Jugged hare	10	Trout with almonds	8
Moules marinière	3	Veal fricassée	9

Don't mistake *nouvelle cuisine* for low calorie preparation. What it gives up in flour it makes up in butter and oil! You can give thanks, though, for the generally smaller portions.

GREEK

Beware of oil in Greek entrées. Greek food is wonderful but not slimming. If you taste oil, add WWUs.

	WWUs		WWUs
Calamari casserole	7	Paprika stew	8
Chicken and pilaf casserole	10	Roast leg of lamb with ouzo	8
Chicken klephti	8	Shish kebab	10
Fish plaki	6	Stifado (beef stew with wine)	10
Greek casserole	12		
Lamb stew	7		

HUNGARIAN

	WWUs		WWUs
Chicken paprika	7	Paprika veal with sour cream sauce	11
Hungarian goulash	9		

INDIAN

Assess your entrée for extra sauces and add WWUs accordingly. The same applies for overly generous portions of Indian food.

	WWUs		WWUs
Beef keema	7	Dansak chicken	8
Beef pasanda	6	Dansak meat	9
Biriani lamb	8	Meat dupiaza	8
Chicken korma	5	Meat vindaloo	8
Chicken pathia	5	Prawn bhuna	5
Chicken rogan gosht	5	Tandoori chicken	4
Chicken tikka marsala	8		

ITALIAN

There are Italian restaurants which serve small portions, and then there are those we know and love which serve enormous portions. Our WWU counts for Italian entrées, e.g. cheese ravioli, are based on an average-size restaurant portion. If you order cheese ravioli frequently in various restaurants, then you know what the average portion looks like. If the serving seems small, use the standard WWU value anyway, to boost your weight loss, but if the portion is larger than usual you must add more WWUs. You can kid yourself, but you can't kid your body. If the cheese ravioli (or anything else), is double the normal size, then it's double the normal WWUs. The laws of mathematics are not open to negotiation.

	WWUs		WWUs
Aubergine, stuffed	7	Pizza, peperoni, ½ of 10″ (26 cm)	6
Baked polenta with pork	9	Potato gnocchi with meat sauce	8
Beef bracciole	5	Risotto con salciccia	10
Cheese gnocchi with tomato sauce	12	Saltimbocca	7
Chicken breasts with prosciutto and cheese	7	Stufato di manzo alla Romana	16
		Steak pizzaiola	9
Chicken cacciatore	8	Veal escalope Florentine	9
Frito misto	13	Veal cutlet	4
Osso buco	10	Veal parmigiana	7
Pizza, anchovy, 10″ (26 cm)	10	Veal piccata	5
Pizza, cheese, 10″ (26 cm)	12	Veal scallopine	5
Pizza, mushroom, ⅛th of 9″ (23 cm)	3	Veal scallopine marsala	5

JEWISH STYLE

	WWUs		WWUs
Blintz, plain, homemade	3	Holishkes, homemade	5
Blintz, vegetable, homemade	4	Meat and carrot tzimmes, homemade	8
Cabbage soup, homemade	7	Noodle apple pudding, homemade	4
Chicken liver, homemade	3		

MEXICAN

	WWUs		WWUs
Arroz con pollo	5	pork, 1	4
Burrito, beef, 1	5	Enchirito	5
chicken, 1	4	Huevos rancheros	8
pork, 1	7	Pintos and cheese	3
Carne asada	5	Quesadilla, 1	4
Chalupas, 1	3	Taco, beef, 1	4
Chilli con carne, 1 mug	3	pork, 1	4
Chilli rellenos	4	Tamale, 1	3
Chorizo, ½ mug	3	Tortilla and cheese	
Chimichanga, beef	5	casserole	9
Enchilada, cheese, 1	5	Tostada, beef	5

SPANISH

It cannot be said too often – the WWU counts for any restaurant entrée are based on the average-size serving. If your plate is heaped higher than usual, add more WWUs!

	WWUs		WWUs
Arroz Catalana	9	Paella (fish)	9
Fritos Mallorcan		Paella Valencia	10
(liver)	8	Suckling pig	13
Mixed grill fish	6		

VEGETABLES, LEGUMES AND STARCHES
(½ mug cooked unless noted)

	WWUs		WWUs
Alfalfa sprouts	0	small, ¼	1
Artichoke, globe, 1	0	purée (guacamole),	
marinated, drained,		½ mug	3
5 hearts	1	Bamboo shoots	0
Artichokes, Jerusalem	0	Beans, baked	2
Asparagus	0	Beans, broad	1
Aubergine	0	butter	2
Avocado, medium	8	green, fresh	0

MAIN COURSES, VEGETABLES AND FRUITS

	WWUs		WWUs
Beans, *cont.*		raw	0
kidney	2	Parsley	0
runner, string or		Parsnip	1
sliced	0	roast	3
Bean sprouts	0	Peas, dried, cooked	2
Beetroot	1	Peas, garden (fresh,	
Broccoli	0	frozen, tinned)	1
Brussels sprouts	0	mange tout	0
Cabbage, green,		marrowfat	
white, red	0	(processed)	2
Calabrese	0	mushy	2
Carrots	0	petit pois	1
Cauliflower	0	Peas pudding	2
Celery	0	Peas, split, cooked	2
Chick peas	4	yellow split, cooked	3
Chicory	0	Peppers, red, yellow,	
Chillies	0	green	0
Chinese leaves	0	Peppers, sweet-pickled	2
Chives	0	Potatoes,	
Corn, cream-style	2	au gratin, with cheese	3
Corn-on-the-cob, 4 oz		baked jacket, 5 oz	
(115 g)	2	(140 g)	1
Courgette	0	baked jacket, large	
Cucumber	0	with butter/cheese	4
Endive	0	boiled, 1 medium	1
Fennel	0	bubble and squeak,	
Garlic	0	homemade, fried	3
Herbs	0	bubble and squeak,	
Kale	0	frozen, grilled	2
Kohlrabi	0	chips, 3½ oz (100 g)	
Leeks	1	homemade	4
Lentils	2	frozen, deep fried	4
Lettuce, all varieties	0	oven-baked	3
Marrow	0	chips, 10,	
Mooli	0	2″ × ½″ × ½″	
Mushrooms	0	(5 × 1 × ½ cm)	2
Mustard and cress	0	croquettes, small, 4	1
Okra	1	large, 1	1
Onions, cooked	1	duchesse, 2	1
creamed	2	instant mash with	

	WWUs		WWUs
Potatoes, *cont.*		Sauerkraut,	
water only	1	unsweetened	0
mashed with milk		Spinach	0
added	1	Spring greens	0
mashed with milk		Spring onions	0
and butter added	2	String beans	0
new, boiled	1	Swede	1
roast, 1 medium	2	buttered, mashed	2
1 small	1	Sweet potatoes, boiled,	
Pumpkin	1	mashed	2
Radishes	0	Tomato paste	2
Ratatouille,		Tomato purée	2
homemade	2	Tomatoes, diced in	
tinned	1	purée	1
Rice, brown or white	1	stewed	1
fried	2	whole, medium, 1	0
pilaf	2	Turnip	0
Rutabaga	1	Water chestnuts, 4	1
Salad cress	0	Watercress	0

FRUITS

	WWUs		WWUs
Apple, baked,		in heavy syrup, 3	
medium, without		medium halves	2
sugar	1	in juice, 3 medium	
Bramley, cooked,		halves	1
unsweetened, 1 mug	1	Banana flakes, ½ mug	3
fresh, whole,		Banana, large	2
medium	1	medium	2
Apple sauce,		small	1
sweetened ½ mug	2	Blackberries, fresh or	
unsweetened, ½		frozen, 1 mug	1
mug	1	Blueberries, fresh or	
Apricots, 8 medium,		frozen, 1 mug	1
fresh	1	Cantaloupe, medium,	
dried, uncooked, 5		½	1
halves	1	Cherries, glacé, 10	2

MAIN COURSES, VEGETABLES AND FRUITS

	WWUs		WWUs
maraschino, 12 large	2	Kumquat, 5–6 medium	1
sour, fresh, ½ mug	1	Lemon, whole	0
sweet, fresh, 20 large	2	Lime, whole	0
Clementines, 2 small	1	Loganberries, fresh, ½ mug	1
Crab apples, fresh, 3½ oz (100 g)	1	in heavy syrup, ½ mug	2
Cranberries, fresh or frozen, ½ mug	1	Lychees, fresh, 3 oz (80 g)	1
Cranberry sauce, 2 tablespooons	1	in syrup, ½ mug	2
Currants, dried, 1 oz (25 g)	1	Mango, fresh, ½ medium	1
Damsons, sweetened, ½ mug	2	Melon balls, sweetened, frozen, ½ mug	2
Dates, block/chopped, 1 oz (25 g)	1	unsweetened, frozen, ½ mug	1
pitted, 8 medium	4	Mixed dried fruit, 1 oz (25 g)	1
Figs, dried or fresh, 1 small	1	Mixed peel, 1 oz (25 g)	1
Fruit cocktail, heavy syrup, ½ mug	2	Nectarine, fresh, medium	1
in juice, ½ mug	1	Orange, whole, fresh, large	2
Ginger, fresh, grated, 1 tablespoon	0	medium	1
Gooseberries, fresh, ½ mug	1	small	1
heavy syrup, ½ mug	2	Orange peel, raw	0
Grapefruit, fresh, ½ medium	1	Orange segments, ½ mug	1
in heavy syrup, ½ mug	2	Passion fruit, 2	1
sections, in juice, ½ mug	1	Paw paw, fresh, ½ medium	1
Grapes, fresh, ½ mug	1	Peach, fresh, 1 medium	1
Greengages, 3	1	in juice, ½ mug	1
Guava, medium	1	Pear, fresh, 1 medium	1
Honeydew melon, ¼ small	1	in juice, ½ mug	1
Kiwi, 2	1	in syrup, ½ mug	2
		Persimmon, medium	1

	WWUs		WWUs
Pineapple, fresh, ½ mug	1	Satsuma	1
in juice, ½ mug	1	Sharon fruit, 1 small	1
in syrup, ½ mug	2	Strawberries, fresh or frozen, ½ mug or 10 large	1
Plums, fresh, 3 medium	1	frozen, sweetened, ½ mug	2
in syrup, ½ mug	2	Sultanas, 1 oz (25 g)	1
Pomegranate, fresh, medium	1	Tangerine, fresh, large	1
Prunes, 4 large	2	Tomato, fresh, large	0
in syrup, 4 medium	3	Toffee apple, 1 medium	4
Quince, fresh, ½ mug	1	Ugli, ½	1
Raisins, dried, 1 oz (25 g)	1	Watermelon, fresh, ½ mug	1
Raspberries, frozen or fresh, ½ mug	1	half slice 6" × 1½" (15 × 4 cm)	2
Rhubarb, cooked, sweetened, ½ mug	2		

· CHAPTER NINE ·

DESSERTS, DAIRY AND BEVERAGES

WWU counting for the dessert, dairy, and beverages categories is easy and straightforward. For beverages, the calories per portion are stated in any calorie list and these calories are easily converted to WWUs. For a mixed drink, we simply totalled the calories for each of the ingredients for any recipe. That is, each WWU contains approximately 75 calories. For mixed drinks, we used the British Standard Weights and Measures.

The dessert count is derived in the same way – from calorie listings and cookbook recipe information.

WWU values for dairy products are worked out directly from calorie lists and are probably the most reliable in this book. In the listing for dairy products we have included milk drinks, all kinds of milk, cream, yogurt and cheese, as well as imitation dairy products.

And so, there you have it. All previous cautions still hold when you eat away from home. To be diet-safe add a few WWUs. The sooner you become familiar with WWU values, the better equipped you are to get on with the business of enjoying the WWD while losing pounds and achieving your goal.

DESSERTS

CAKES
(2 oz/50 g portion unless noted)

	WWUs
Almond cake	3
Angel cake	3
Angel sandwich cake, 1½ oz (40 g)	4
Apple slice, 1	3
Bakewell tart, individual	3
slice	4
Banana cake, ⅙ of 9" (23 cm) cake	3
Battenberg, 1 slice	3
Black forest gâteau	4
Brownies, chocolate, 1 square	3
Butterfly buns, 1	3
Caramel Shortcake, 1	2
Cheesecake (¼ medium, frozen)	3
Chelsea bun	3
Chocolate cake, rich, butter iced	6
Chocolate coated mini roll	2
Chocolate coated swiss roll	4
Chocolate crispie, 1	3
Chocolate cup cake, 1	1
Chocolate sandwich cake	4
Chorley cakes, 1	4
Christmas cake	4
Coconut cake	4
Currant bun, 1	2
Dairy Cream Gâteau (Birds Eye, ⅕)	3

	WWUs
Dairy Cream Sponge, (Birds Eye, ⅕)	3
Dundee cake	3
Eccles cake, 1	3
Fondant Fancies, 1	2
Florentines	4
Fruit Sundae, 1	3
Genoa Cherry, iced	3
Gingerbread, homemade, 3" (8 cm) square	4
Golden syrup cake, ⅙	3
Jamaica Ginger, ⅙	3
Jam Swiss Roll, 1½ oz (40 g)	2
Madeira	4
Madelines, 1	2
Marble cake	3
Parkin	3
Rock cakes	2
Sultana cake	3
Victoria sandwich, 3 egg, homemade, jam filled, ⅛	5
butter cream filling, ⅛	7
butter cream iced, ⅛	8
glacé iced, ⅛	6

BISCUITS

	WWUs
Abbey crunch, 1	1
Albany, 2	1
All butter crunch, 2	1
Apricot date bar, 1	1
Arrowroot thin, 2	1

DESSERTS, DAIRY AND BEVERAGES

	WWUs		WWUs
Assorted biscuits/ wafers, 1	1	Gingerbread men, 1	2
Bandit, 1	2	Ginger nuts, 1	1
Barbary, 1	1	Ginger thins, 3	1
Bourbon, 1	1	Ginger snaps, 2	1
Braemar, 1	1	Gipsy creams, 1	2
Brandysnap, 1	1	Granola, 1	1
Butter crinkle, 2	1	Hob nobs, 1	1
Butter crunch cream, 1	1	Jaffa cakes, 1	1
Butter Osborne, 2	1	Jam sandwich biscuit, 1	1
Caramel wafers, 1	2	Kit Kat, 2 fingers	2
Choc O lait, 1	1	4 fingers	4
Chocolate chip cookies, 1	1	Macaroons, 1	2
Chocolate crispies, 1	2	Marie, 2	1
Chocolate cup cakes, 1	2	Mallows (chocolate coated), 1	1
Chocolate digestives, McVities, 1	2	Malted milk, 2	1
other brands, 1	1	Muesli bars, 1	2
Chocolate filled wafers, 2	1	Nice biscuits, 1	2
Chocolate fingers, 2	1	Oatmeal biscuits, 1	1
Chocolate nut cookies, 1	1	Penguin, 1	2
Chocolate orange cookies, 1	1	Petite beurre, 3	1
		Princess biscuits, 1	1
		Priory biscuits, 1	1
		Rich tea fingers, 1	1
		Ring mallows, 1	1
Chocolate sandwich cakes, 1	2	Royal Scot biscuits, 1	1
Chocolate tea cakes, 1	1	Shortbread fingers, 1	2
Chocolate Vienna, 1	1	Shortcake, 1	1
Club, 1	2	Shorties, 1	1
Cocoa crispies, 1	1	Sponge fingers, 3	1
Currant crisp, 2	1	Tea biscuits, plain, 3	1
Custard creams, 1	1	chocolate topped, 1	1
Digestive plain, 1	1	Wafercreams, 1	2
Fig rolls, 1	1	Wafers (ice cream), 12	1
Florentines, 1	3	Waffles, 1	1
Fruit shortcake, 1	1	Wholemeal bran, 1	1
Garibaldi, 2	1	Yo-Yo, 1	2

ICE CREAM
(1 mug unless noted)
(2 scoops = ⅙ litre approx.)

	WWUs
Chocolate ice cream	3
⅙ litre	2
Chocolate rich/ homemade	5
Cornish dairy family brick, ¼	4
	2
Cornish ice cream bar	2
Diet ice cream, 1 small scoop (70 ml) portion	1
Individual (Wall's) slice	1
Lyons Maid family brick, ¼	2
Neapolitan, 1 slice	3
⅙ litre	2
Raspberry, strawberry	3
Tutti frutti, ⅙ litre	4
Vanilla, ⅙ litre	2
Soft easy scoop	3
Sorbet	3
⅙ litre	2

SPECIALITY ICE CREAM

	WWUs
Arctic Gâteau, ⅕	2
Arctic Log, ⅙	2
Arctic Roll, ⅙	1
Baked Alaska, 3 oz (80 g)	3
Chocolate coated vanilla ice cream	2
Cone/wafer	1
Cornetto	3
Cornish choc sundae	2

	WWUs
Frozen mousse, 1	2
Funny faces	1
Funny feet	2
Ice cream sandwich	2
King cones	3
Lolly ices	1
Lolly ice with ice cream centre	2
Popsicle, chocolate	2
fruit flavour	1

PIES
(¼ of 7" [18 cm] or ⅙ of 8" [20 cm] pie unless noted)

	WWUs
Apple, frozen, cooked	4
homemade	4
Bakewell tart	4
Blackberry cheesecake	5
Butterscotch, homemade	6
Custard tart	3
individual	2
Custard slice	3
Dutch apple slice	3
French apple flan	4
Fruit pies	4
individual, large	5
individual, small	3
Fruit puff pastries	3
Jam tart, individual small	2
Lemon chiffon, homemade	4
Lemon curd tarts, individual	2
Lemon meringue, homemade	4

DESSERTS, DAIRY AND BEVERAGES

	WWUs		WWUs
Mince pie, large	3	Lemon soufflé,	
small	2	homemade	3
with puff pastry	3	Pudding Instant	
Pie crust, baked, 1 9″		mix, vanilla fruit	2
(23 cm) shell	12	Rice pudding	2
Treacle tart, ¼ 6″		Tapioca cream	3
(15 cm) tart	3	Zabaglione	2
small individual	2		

PUDDINGS, MOUSSES AND JELLIES
(½ mug, unless noted)

	WWUs
Angel Delight	2
Apple snow	2
Baked custard	3
Blancmange	2
Bread pudding with raisins	4
Caramel custard	4
Cheesecake, individual	3
Chocolate Cream Supreme	2
Chocolate pudding, from mix	2
Chocolate Super Mousse tub	2
Creamed macaroni	2
Creamed Sago	2
Custard	2
Fruit Supreme	2
Fruit soufflé	3
Instant Whip	2
Jelly, fruit flavour	1
fruit flavoured, with fruit	2
Jelly Creams	2
Junket	1

OTHER

	WWUs
Apple brown betty, ½ mug	2
Apple puff pastries	3
Apple sponge, ½ mug	3
Apple strudel	3
Black cherry and Buttercream roll, ⅙	2
Black forest gâteau, slice	5
Bread and Butter pudding, ½ mug	3
Chocolate sponge pudding	4
Christmas pudding 3 oz (80 g)	3
Cream choux puff with custard filling	4
with whipped cream	4
Danish pastry, fruit-filled, 4½″ (11 cm)	4
plain, 4½″ (11 cm)	4
Doughnut, 3¾″ (10 cm)	3
Eclair, custard-filled, chocolate icing, 5″ × 2″ (13 × 5 cm)	3
Eve's pudding, homemade	4

	WWUs		WWUs
Fruit crumble	4	Syrup sponge	
Fruit pie filling, ¼ jar	1	pudding, 3 oz (80 g)	5
Fruit sponge, Tiffany's	2	Treacle pudding, 3 oz (80 g)	4
Jam roly poly, ¼ Tiffany's	4	Trifle, homemade, ½ mug	3
Peach cobbler	2	homemade with cream, ½ mug	4
Profiteroles, 1	2	small tub	2
Rum babas, 3 oz (80 g)	3	small tub with cream	4
with cream	4		
Suet pudding, 3 oz (80 g)	4		

DAIRY

CHEESE

(1 oz/25 g unless noted)

The values expressed for hard and semi-soft cheeses are based on their high fat content.

	WWUs		WWUs
Blue or Roquefort	2	Cream	2
Boursin	2	Edam	2
Brie	2	Emmental	2
Caerphilly	2	Feta	2
Cambozola	2	Gouda	2
Camembert	2	Gruyère	2
Cheddar	2	Lancashire	2
Cheese spread	2	Leicester	2
Cheshire	2	Lymeswold	2
Cottage, low-fat,		Mozzarella	2
2½ oz (70 g)	1	Münster	2
diet 3 oz (80 g)	1	Neufchâtel	2
with cucumber/prawn/cheddar 2 oz (50 g)	1	Parmesan	2
		Parmesan, grated, 1 tablespoon	1
with onions/peppers/pineapple 3 oz (80 g)	1	Philadelphia	2
		Port Salut	2
		Processed	2

DESSERTS, DAIRY AND BEVERAGES

	WWUs
Quark, low fat	1
Ricotta	1
Stilton	2
Swiss	2
Wensleydale	2

MILK

	WWUs
Channel Island, 1 mug (8 fl oz/225 ml)	3
Condensed, sweet, tinned, 1 mug	13
Dry, skimmed, ⅓ mug	1
skimmed with vegetable fat, ¼ mug	4
whole, ¼ mug	3
Evaporated, tinned, 1 mug	4
Semi-skimmed	2
Skimmed	1
Whole, ⅓ mug	1
1 mug	2

CREAM
(1 mug, 8 fl oz/225 ml)

	WWUs
Clotted cream	14
1 tablespoon	3
Cornish cream	14
1 tablespoon	3
Devon cream	14
1 tablespoon	3
Double	13
1 tablespoon	2
Extra thick	9
1 tablespoon	2

	WWUs
Extra thick double	13
1 tablespoon	2
Half	4
2 tablespoons	1
Non dairy	9
1 tablespoon	2
Single	7
1 tablespoon	1
Soured	7
1 tablespoon	1
Spooning	11
1 tablespoon	2
Tinned cream	7
1 tablespoon	1
Whipped aerosol, 1 tablespoon	1
5 tablespoons	1
Whipping	11
1 tablespoon	2

MILK DRINKS
(1 mug)

	WWUs
Banana, low fat, milk drink	2
Bournvita	3
Chocolate milk	3
Chocolate Milk Drink, low fat	2
Cocoa, sweetened	4
Coconut water	1
Drinking chocolate	4
Egg nog	4
Goats' milk	2
Horlicks	3
Milkshake,	
commercial mix	2
fast-food restaurant	4
homemade	4

	WWUs		WWUs
Nesquick, made up	1	Fruit yogurt	2
Soya bean milk	2	Greek style (1 mug)	4
Strawberry milk drink,		Low fat, plain	2
low fat	2	Munch brunch	2
		Shape yogurt	1
		Thick and creamy	3
		Whole milk, plain	
		(homemade)	2

YOGURT
(5.3 oz/145 g unless noted)

	WWUs
Diet (very low fat)	1

BEVERAGES

BEER AND CIDER
(½ pint/10 fl oz/300 ml unless noted)

	WWUs		WWUs
Ale, brown	2	Lager	2
pale	2	canned, 15 fl oz	
strong	3	(440 ml)	2
Barley wine	3	non alcoholic	1
Beer, canned, 15 fl oz		Perry	2
(440 ml)	2	Pomagne, dry	2
Bitter, canned	2	sweet	3
draught	2	Shandy	2
keg	2	low calorie	1
Cider, dry	2	Stout, bottled	2
special reserve dry	2	extra	2
special reserve sweet	3		
sweet	2		
vintage	4		
Draught,			
home brewed	2		
mild	1		

SPIRITS, LIQUEURS AND SYRUPS
(⅙ gill/1 fl oz approx./25 ml)

Spirits 70° proof/40% with ice, water, soda or low calorie mixers.

	WWUs
Advocaat	1

DESSERTS, DAIRY AND BEVERAGES

	WWUs
Anisette	1
Armagnac	1
B & B	2
Benedictine	2
Bourbon	1
Brandy	1
Brandy liqueur	2
Campari	1
Calvados	1
Cassis	1
Chartreuse	2
Cherry brandy	1
Crême d'apricot	1
Crême de cacao	2
Crême de cassis	1
Crême de menthe	2
Cognac	1
Cointreau	1
Curaçao	2
Drambuie	2
Galliano	1
Gin	1
Grand marnier	2
Grenadine syrup	2
Irish creme	2
Kirsch	1
Malibu	1
Ouzo	1
Pernod	1
Rum	1
100° proof	2
Southern Comfort	1
Sloe gin	2
Tia maria	2
Tequilla	1
Vodka	1
Whisky	1
90° proof	2

FORTIFIED WINES/SHORTS
(⅓ gill/2 fl oz approx./45 ml)

	WWUs
Campari	2
Cinzano	2
Dubonnet	1
Irish Velvet	3
Madeira	1
Martini bianco	2
Dry	1
Rosé	2
Rosso	2
Port, dry	1
Fine Old Ruby	1
Special Reserve	2
Sherry, cream/milk	2
dry	1
medium dry	1
sweet	2
Vermouth, dry	1
non alcoholic	1
sweet	2

WINE
(4 fl oz/115 ml measure)

	WWUs
Champagne, 1 glass	1
Red wine, dry, 1 glass	1
medium, 1 glass	1
Rosé, 1 glass	1
Spritzer (½ measure wine and soda)	1
White wine, dry, 1 glass	1
medium, 1 glass	1
sparkling, 1 glass	1
sweet, 1 glass	2

MIXED DRINKS

Using British Standard Weights and Measures for spirits (based on 1 measure of base spirit(s))

	WWUs
Bacardi cocktail	2
Bloody Mary	2
Brandy egg nog	5
Bucks fizz	2
Champagne cocktail	3
Cuba libre	3
Daiquiri	2
Gin and tonic	3
Gin fizz	2
Highball, with mixer	2
Manhattan, dry vermouth	2
sweet vermouth	2
Margarita	2
Martini, dry, extra dry, medium	2
sweet	2
Mint julep	3
Piña colada	4
Pink lady	2
Planter's punch	3
Port flip	4
Rob Roy	2
Rum sour	2
Screwdriver	3
Side car	2
Sloe gin fizz	3
Sombrero	2
Stinger	3
Tom Collins	3
Vodka and tonic	3
Vodka Collins	2
Vodka sour	2
Whisky sour	2

COFFEE AND TEA

Coffee and tea, black, no sugar, or sweetened, with artificial sweeteners have a WWU of 0. All cup sizes, unless noted.

	WWUs
Coffee, black	0
Coffee, 1 cup, black, with 1–3 teaspoons sugar	1
1 cup, ½ fl oz (13 ml) cream	1
1 cup, ½ fl oz (13 ml) cream, 1–3 teaspoons sugar	1
1 cup, ½ fl oz (13 ml) milk, 1–3 teaspoons sugar	1
1 cup, 1–2 teaspoons non-dairy creamer	1
1–2 teaspoons non-dairy creamer, 1–3 teaspoons sugar	1
Irish	1
Espresso, unsweetened	1
sweetened	2
Herbal teas	0
Tea, ½ fl oz (13 ml) milk, and 1–3 teaspoons sugar	1
+ lemon	0
Tea mix, lemon, sweetened	1
mix with or without lemon, no sugar	0

SOFT DRINKS
(11 fl oz/330 ml unless noted)

All sugar-free diet drinks have a WWU of 0.

	WWUs
Bitter lemon	2
6 fl oz (170 ml)	1
Cactus Cooler	3
Cherryade	2
Coca-Cola	2
6 fl oz (170 ml)	2
Cola, other brand names	2
6 fl oz (170 ml)	2
Cream soda	2
Dandelion & Burdock	2
Fruit-flavoured fizzy drinks	2
Ginger ale	2
Ginger beer	2
Iron brew	2
Lemonade	2
Lilt	2
6 fl oz (170 ml)	1
Limeade	2
Lucozade	3
Orangeade	2
Pepsi	2
Quatro	2
Seven-up	2
Shandy	2
6 fl oz (170 ml)	1
low calorie	1
Sprite	2
Squirt	2
Tango	2
Tizer	2
Tonic water	2
Top deck	2
Vimto	2
6 fl oz (170 ml)	1

FRUIT JUICES AND DRINKS
(½ mug/4 fl oz/115 ml unless noted)

	WWUs
Apple juice, unsweetened	1
Apricot juice, unsweetened	1
Apricot nectar	1
Blackcurrant drink (Ribena) 4 tablespoons in 1 mug water	3
Blackcurrant with apple juice	1
Carrot juice, 1 mug	1
Grapefruit juice, unsweetened, 1 mug	1
sweetened, 1 mug	1
Grape juice	1
Lemon and lime, 4 tablespoons in 1 mug water	2
Lemon barley, 4 tablespoons in 1 mug water	1
Lemon juice, 1 mug	1
Lime cordial (Roses), 4 tablespoons in 1 mug water	2
Lime juice, fresh	1
Mineral water with apple juice (Piermont), 1 mug	1

	WWUs		WWUs
Mixed citrus juice, unsweetened	1	Rise and Shine, diluted	2
Mixed fruit juice, unsweetened	1	Rose hip syrup, 4 tablespoons in 1 mug water	3
Moonshine	1	Squash, 4 tablespoons in 1 mug water	2
Orange 'C', sweetened	1	Squash, diabetic, lemon, 4 tablespoons in 1 mug water	0
Orange juice fresh, unsweetened	1		
sweetened	1		
Orange juice drink	1		
Orange concentrate, diluted, frozen	1	Squash, diabetic orange, 4 tablespoons in 1 mug water	1
Orange juice dried, diluted, sweetened	2		
Orange-grapefruit juice, sweetened	2	Squash, low calorie, 4 tablespoons in 1 mug water	1
Peach nectar	1		
Pineapple juice, sweetened	1	Tomato juice, 1 mug	1
unsweetened	1	Tomato juice cocktail, 1 mug	1
Prune juice, sweetened	2		
unsweetened, ⅓ mug	1	Tropical fruit juice	1

· CHAPTER TEN ·

DIETING SEVEN DAYS A WEEK: THE FLEXI-DIET

Some diets work for some people some of the time; no diet works for all of the people all the time. We are not all alike. Our tastes and lifestyles vary greatly. We diet differently and we lose weight differently. Is it any wonder, then, that in the weight-loss marketplace there are so many diets to choose from? In this chapter we offer you an alternative.

Where do diets come from?

From the paintings of the 18th and 19th centuries, you'll notice that the full figure – especially for women – was the fashion. A plump body was a sign of affluence and social distinction, therefore admired. Today it is neither healthy, admirable nor fashionable to be overweight. On the contrary. There is nothing less true than everybody loves a fat man or woman.

Although it is probable that obesity took the same toll on health and longevity then as it does today, in past centuries the connection between fat and physical ills was not made. Not until the 20th century was obesity considered a disease or given wide medical attention.

Before that time, however, in 1881 there was at least one man who experimented and cured a specific illness through weight loss. This man was Dr William Harvey, an English ear surgeon. One of his patients, William Banting, came to him with an earache. After careful examination of the corpulent, hard-of-hearing, 60 year old Banting, Dr Harvey concluded that there was no disease and no sign of infection. He wondered if the excess fat was causing pressure on Banting's inner ear and thereby causing the earache.

Dr Harvey put Banting on an unorthodox diet of venison, poultry, fish and a limited amount of alcohol. No sugars or starches were permitted. One year later William Banting weighed in 46 pounds (20 kg) lighter and had perfect hearing. Flushed with success, William Banting published his own version of Dr Harvey's diet and called it the Banting Diet. This diet was the first published weight-loss diet and was the forerunner of the high-protein, low-carbohydrate diets that followed in later years.

The next major diet phase focused on calorie counting. By 1930 doctors believed that excess food intake converted to excess fat. Even then it was recognised that some foods provided higher calories per serving than others. Obviously, puddings, cakes and sweets were denser in calories than fruits, vegetables and certain proteins. The reducing diets of the 1930s emphasised the importance of calories alone. The idea was to eat as few of them as possible. The calorie-counting theory ravished Britain and America, and calorie-counter books proliferated. No thought was given to the value of a particular food *per se*, nor to what it did or did not contribute to the body's total health. So people ate whatever foods they pleased as they counted their calories. Some people lost weight. Some people gained weight.

The course of diet history changed drastically in the late 1950s when Norman Joliffe, MD, conceived the Prudent Men's Diet for members of an anticoronary club in New York. Members of this group were middle-aged men, considered to be predisposed to coronary disease when they joined. The Prudent Diet Dr Joliffe designed for them advocated neither excessive use of, nor complete abstention from, any one food. It did, however, limit intake of fatty meats, high-fat dairy products, eggs, hydrogenated fats (e.g. margarine) and foods containing any of these ingredients. After following the Prudent Diet for some time, their bodies slimmed down, their blood pressure decreased, and the expected rate of heart attacks was cut in half.

At this time Dr Joliffe was the director of the Bureau of Nutrition of the Department of Health in New York. From the feedback he received from the members of his anticoronary club he formulated a new type of reducing plan. His New York City Diet balanced proteins, carbohydrates and fats within a calorie limit, 1,200 calories for women and 1,500 calories for men.

For the first time in history there was a recommended, easy-to-live-with diet on which people could lose weight. This successful plan was adopted by many weight-loss groups and clubs. And, finally, without suffering or starvation, many people were reaching their weight goals.

I was one of those people who experienced success by following a well-balanced eating plan that provided 1,200 calories per day. After trying every fad diet that had come across the Brooklyn Bridge, in 1965, at 32 years of age, I finally shed my puppy fat.

I've been asked many times as to the motivation behind my trying one more diet. And there are as many reasons as there are ingredients in any perfected recipe, but one incident does stand out in my mind as the push behind my new start. It happened at my weekly bridge game through the intervention of my friends. It was one of the most humiliating experiences of my life. I was asked to sit down and to listen. Then, as they all faced me, one of my friends said, 'We're all worried about you. You're growing and growing. It looks as though each week you come to the game, you stop at the petrol station first and get yourself pumped full of air. We're afraid you're going to burst. Please, you've got to *do* something with yourself.'

So I did something with myself. That week I went to a local diet group. I followed the up-dated New York City Diet, and it worked! I worked! I lost over one-third of myself – more than 40 pounds (18 kg). I was thrilled. At last I was free of the fat in which I'd been encased for far too long, and finally I could get on with my life.

In the evangelical glow of my enthusiasm I believed that I could help everyone in the world to get thin. It was with that great goal and that energy and zeal that I dedicated myself to helping others lose weight by founding The Diet Workshop.

The Diet Workshop is unique in the weight-loss field because our mission is to teach healthy eating habits not only for weight loss but also forever. Losing weight is never an easy process, but we meet people halfway with our innovative programme. Further, it's our philosophy that once you've accomplished your weight loss, there is nothing in life you can't accomplish, within reason.

A more flexible system

I have explained The Wild Weekend Diet, but at The Diet Workshop we recognise that it may not suit everyone all the time. You may find a more flexible system through the week would suit your lifestyle better. If you are eating canteen meals, or go on holiday, need a change or do not take kindly to a very rigid diet throughout the week, read on.

Our more flexible diet we call The Flexi-Diet. It is also based on the New York Diet, allowing 8,400 calories per week for women and 10,500 for men, and recommending a variety of food choices and a balanced diet which includes protein and carbohydrates at each meal.

The Flexi-Diet differs from The Wild Weekend Diet in that it has two parts: the basic compulsory section – the Core – and the Flexi which provides the choice. The Core Diet dictates the first 850 calories and the dieter chooses her or his own remaining food to bring the daily total up to 1,200 calories for women and 1,500 for men. The calorie intake is the same for each of the seven days of the week. You are not saving up for a Wild Weekend but can choose a few favourites every day.

The Flexi-Diet has a special advantage. Since you have to take a greater responsibility for choosing your food and controlling your choices daily, you actually learn how to maintain your weight loss from your very first day of dieting.

The Flexi-Diet is an alternative to the Wild Weekend Diet if you like to have treats every day. Every day is a wild day! For those of you who want to diet seven days a week and learn healthy eating habits for a lifetime of thinness, this is the way to do it.

The Flexi-Diet offers you a world of food choices high in nutrition, highly satisfying, yet calorie-controlled. Even the compulsory Core Diet gives choices from each of these six categories: Protein, Bread, Lo Vegetables, Hi Vegetables, Milk and Fruit. And you will also have daily your choice of Flexi-Units. In fact, all choices – Core and Flexi – are broken down into units.

The chart below shows how The Core Diet works. We explain later how you will use your Flexi-Units and how many you have.

THE CORE DIET

BREAKFAST	LUNCH	DINNER
1 Protein Unit	3 Protein Units	4 Protein Units
1 Grain Unit	1 Grain Unit	1 Hi Vegetable Unit
	Lo Vegetables	Lo Vegetables

Daily: 1 Dairy Unit, 2 Fruit Units (1 citrus), and Flexi-Units. *Any time:* Artificial sweetener, bouillon, coffee, diet beverages, 1 tablespoon diet dressing, diet gelatine, 2 teaspoons diet jam, herbs, lemon, lime, Lo Vegetables, mustard, pepper, salt, soy sauce, spices, tea, vinegar, water, Worcestershire sauce.

The following are lists of the six categories. An asterisk indicates the lowest-calorie foods in each category; a dagger indicates high fibre.

UNITS FOR THE CORE DIET

PROTEIN

1 oz (25 g) cooked = 1 Unit, unless noted

Cheeses	Edam
*Cottage, 2 oz (50 g)	Cheddar

(Limit, 4 oz/115 g per week)

Ricotta   legs
Chicken   *breast
  whole   Egg

(Limit, 4 per week)

*Finnan Haddock   *Tofu
*Fish, white   Trout
Liver   Tuna, drained
Salmon, canned or fresh   oil-packed
*Shellfish   *brine-packed
  Crab   Turkey
  Mussels   *breast
  Prawns   dark meat
  Scallops   Veal

Limit to 3 meals weekly:

Beef   Lamb
Frankfurters   Pork
Ham   Tongue

BREAD AND GRAIN

Bread   French bread
  Plain, 1 oz (25 g)   Rye crispbread
  †Wholemeal, 1 oz (25 g)   Muffin
Bulgar, cooked, ¼ cup   Plain, ½
Breakfast cereal, cold,   †Wholemeal, ½
  unsugared, ⅔ oz (17 g)   Pitta bread, 1 oz (25 g)
†Cereal, oats cooked, 4 fl oz   Roll, 1 oz (25 g)
  (115 g)

Choose at least 1 whole grain serving per day.

LO VEGETABLES

(Any quantity or time as desired)

†Asparagus   Bamboo shoots
Aubergine   Bean sprouts

Broccoli
†Brussels sprouts
†Cabbage
†Carrots
†Cauliflower
Celery
Chicory
Chinese leaves
Courgettes
Cucumber
Fennel
†Green beans
Lettuce
Marrow

†Mushrooms
†Onion, raw
†Peppers
Pickles, dill
Pimientos
Radishes
Sauerkraut
Spinach
†Spring greens
Spring onions
†String beans
†Tomato
Watercress

HI VEGETABLES
(½ mug = 1 unit unless noted)

†*Artichoke (globe)
Artichoke (Jerusalem)
Beetroot
Celeriac
Corn, ½ ear or ½ mug
Kidney beans, ⅓ mug
Leek
Lima beans, ⅓ mug
Mixed frozen vegetables
Okra
†*Onion, cooked

Parsnip
†Peas
†Potato, small, baked or boiled
Pumpkin
Swede
Tomato purée
Tomato sauce
Turnip
Vegetable juice, 12 fl oz (350 ml)

DAIRY

Semi skimmed milk, 6 fl oz (170 ml)
Skimmed milk, 8 fl oz (225 ml)

Skimmed milk powder, 4 level tablespoons
Yogurt, low fat, plain, 8 fl oz (225 ml)

FRUIT

(1 mug = 8 fl oz)

Apple, medium size	*Nectarine, medium size
Apricot, 3 small	Orange, medium size
Banana, ½	*Peach, medium size
*Berries, any kind, ½ mug	Pear, medium size
*Cantaloupe, ½ small	*Pineapple
Cherries, fresh, 10	tinned in own juice, ½ mug
Figs, fresh, 1	
*Fruit, in own juice, ½ mug	fresh, ½ mug
*Grapefruit, ½	*Plums, 2 small
Grapes, ½ mug	Prunes, 3
Honeydew, 2″ (5 cm) wedge	Tangerine, medium size
Juice, unsweetened, ½ mug	Tomato juice, 1 mug
Kiwi fruit, 2	Watermelon, 1 mug
Mango, medium, ½	

All fruits except juices are good choices for high fibre

Core eating

On The Core Diet Plan you choose 1 Protein Unit and 1 Bread Unit for breakfast. Select these as you wish from the two relevant sections. We recommend you choose at least 1 wholegrain serving per day.

For lunch you might choose a variety of protein foods to make up your 3 Protein Units, i.e. 4 oz (115 g) cottage cheese and 1 oz (25 g) prawns. You will add to this your chosen bread unit and any vegetables you like from the Lo Vegetable selection. Then for the evening meal you have 4 Protein Units, 1 Hi Vegetable Unit and any Lo Vegetable you wish.

Each day on The Core Diet you will also select 1 Milk Unit and 2 Fruit Units to have at any time. One of your fruits must be citrus – 1 orange or ½ grapefruit.

In addition you will have the pleasure of your Flexi Units.

Flexi units

It is these units that make The Flexi-Diet fun and interesting, providing you with a more varied diet from which to choose. The Flexi-Units are sub-divided into three groups: CORE, MORE, and YOUR. These are gradually added to your diet. The following chart shows how these are slowly introduced.

DAILY FLEXI UNIT ALLOWANCE

These are the **extras** you are allowed on top of the basic Core Diet. Food may be added to meals or eaten at any time.

Week 1:	Women	None (Core Diet only)
	Men	None (Core Diet only)
Week 2:	Women	1–5 CORE Flexi Units
	Men	5–8 CORE Flexi Units
Week 3:	Women	1–5 CORE or MORE Flexi Units
	Men	5–8 CORE or MORE Flexi Units
Thereafter:	Women	1–5 CORE, MORE or YOUR Flexi Units
	Men	5–8 CORE, MORE or YOUR Flexi Units

CORE Flexi Units
Turn back to page 165 for the list of Core Units. You may select your units from these lists:

PROTEIN	DAIRY
BREAD AND GRAINS	FRUIT
HI VEGETABLES	

These you can choose in any combination you wish. If you want to enjoy lots of fruit or crave bread, then choose your units from these CORE lists. Foods in the Lo Vegetables lists are of course free for you to choose any time.

MORE Flexi Units
These widen your choice and include many favourite foods. By the third week of your diet you may include any of these as an alternative to Core Diet foods. MORE Flexi Units are:

GRAINS

Barley, dry, 4 teaspoons
Bran, ¼ cup
Cornmeal cooked, ½ mug
Cornflour, 2 tablespoons
Flour, 2 tablespoons
Macaroni, cooked, ½ mug
Matzo, ½ piece
Noodles, cooked, ½ mug
Raisin bread, 1 oz (25 g)
Rice, white or brown, hot, cooked, ½ mug
Rice, wild, cooked, ⅓ mug
Rice cakes, 2
Rusks, 5 (16 calories each)
Spaghetti, cooked, ½ mug
Taco shells, 2
Tortilla, 1
Wheat germ, 2 tablespoons

PROTEIN

Bacon, lean, back, ¾ oz (20 g)
Herring, kippered or pickled, 1 oz (25 g)
Liverwurst, ¾ oz (20 g)
Mackerel, smoked, 1 oz (25 g)

LEGUMES

Beans, baked, ¼ mug
  kidney, cooked, ⅓ mug
  lima, cooked, ⅓ mug
Chick peas, 2 tablespoons
Lentils, cooked, ⅓ mug

DAIRY

Cream, double, 1½ tablespoons
Cream, single, 3 tablespoons
Cream, whipping, 2 tablespoons
Cream cheese, whipped, 2 tablespoons
Milk, whole, ⅓ mug
Yogurt, fruit, ½ carton
  fruit, diet 1 carton
  very low fat, 1 carton

HI VEGETABLES

Avocado, small, ¼
Potato, sweet, ½
Spaghetti sauce (tomato), ⅓ mug

FRUIT

Cherries, maraschino, 6
Dates, pitted, 2
Figs, dried, 1
Fruit cocktail, juice packed, ½ mug
Persimmon, medium
Pomegranate, medium
Raisins, 1 oz

FATS
Limit 2 selections daily

Butter, 2 teaspoons
Low fat spread, 1 tablespoon
Margarine, 2 teaspoons
Margarine, soft, whipped, 1 tablespoon
Mayonnaise, 2 teaspoons
Oil, polyunsaturated
  Corn, 2 teaspoons
  Safflower, 2 teaspoons
  Sunflower, 2 teaspoons

NUTS

Almonds, whole in shell, 12
Coconut, fresh or dried, shredded, ¼ mug
Cashews, roasted, 4
Peanuts, roasted in shell, ½ oz (12 g)
  raw, shelled, 25
Macadamia, roasted, 3
Pistachio, in shell, 15

SEEDS

Pumpkin, shelled, ½ oz (12 g)
Sesame, ½ oz (12 g)
Sunflower, ½ oz (12 g)

DRINKS

Beer, 8 fl oz (225 ml)
Beer, light, 12 fl oz (350 ml)
Bourbon, 1 fl oz (25 ml)
Champagne, 3 fl oz (80 ml)
Gin, 1 fl oz (25 ml)
Rum, 1 fl oz (25 ml)
Scotch whisky, 1 fl oz (25 ml)
Vodka, 1 fl oz (25 ml)
Wine, dry, red or white, 3 fl oz (80 ml)

EXTRAS

Chewing gum, regular or sugarless, 8 sticks
Cocoa, plain, 2 tablespoons
Cranberry sauce, 2 tablespoons
Hamburger relish, 2 tablespoons
Peanut butter, 2 teaspoons
Popcorn, commercial, unsweetened, 3 mugs
Popcorn, home prepared, 2 mugs
Seafood cocktail sauce, ¼ cup
Soup, meatless, non-creamed, ¾ cup
Tonic water, 6 fl oz (170 ml)
Whipped topping, non-dairy, ¼ mug

YOUR Flexi-Units

So far on The Core Diet there have been many of your favourite food and drinks you have had to forgo. Once you arrive at the fourth week on this diet you can include YOUR own choice of foods. Any food or drink in the world YOU want you can include in YOUR diet so long as you count unit value.

These are YOUR own choice of foods. Browse through Chapters 7, 8 and 9 and choose what YOU would like with a unit value of 1.1 Wild Weekend Unit = 1 of YOUR Flexi-Units = maximum of 75 calories. So long as you have followed The Flexi-Diet for at least three weeks you can now make YOUR diet more fun and a little wild.

When you feel ready – perhaps when you want to maintain

your present weight – you can select YOUR Flexi-Units. If you can't find your favourite food on our lists, check the packaging; it may tell you how many calories it contains and you can then work out its unit value.

At The Diet Workshop we believe that the diet you will stay on the longest and be the most successful on is the diet that you design for yourself.

You'll continue to lose weight as long as you stay within the Core Diet and restrict your total Flexi-Unit intake to 5 if you're a woman, 8 if you're a man. This holds true no matter from which Flexi-Unit list you choose your foods.

The following are some sample menus which will show you how to follow the Flexi-Diet correctly.

Sample Core Diet

Here's a sample Week One menu of the Core Diet with no Flexi-Units. It does contain 'Add Daily' 2 Fruit Units and 1 Dairy Unit, all of which are marked with an asterisk so you can see where they are used.

WEEK ONE

CORE DIET	SAMPLE CORE MENU (*no Flexi-Units*)
Breakfast	
1 Protein Unit	1 scrambled egg
1 Grain Unit	1 small slice wholemeal toast
	*½ mug grapefruit juice
Lunch	
3 Protein Units	3 oz (80 g) tuna, brine-packed
1 Grain Unit	1 oz (25 g) wholemeal bread
1 Lo Vegetable Unit	Lettuce and cucumber

DIETING SEVEN DAYS A WEEK: THE FLEXI-DIET

CORE DIET	SAMPLE CORE MENU *(no Flexi-Units)*
Dinner	
4 Protein Units 1 Lo Vegetable Unit 1 Hi Vegetable Unit	4 oz (115 g) grilled chicken 1 mug cauliflower ½ mug beetroot or 1 small jacket potato
Daily	
*1 Dairy Unit *2 Fruit Units (1 citrus)	Milk-shake: Blend together *1 mug skimmed milk. *½ mug frozen, unsweetened strawberries, artificial sweetener.

WEEK TWO (A)

The following is a sample menu of the Core Diet. It includes 3 *CORE* Flexi-Units which are marked + 1. The daily Fruit and Dairy Units are marked with an *.

CORE DIET	SAMPLE CORE MENU PLUS 3 Flexi-Units
Breakfast	
1 Protein Unit 1 Grain Unit	1 scrambled egg ½ small slice wholemeal toast *½ mug grapefruit juice

CORE DIET   SAMPLE CORE MENU
                                               PLUS 3 Flexi-Units

Lunch

3 Protein Units	4 oz (115 g) tuna, brine-packed + 1
1 Grain Unit	1 pitta bread + 1
1 Lo Vegetable Unit	Lettuce and cucumber
	*10 fresh cherries

Dinner

4 Protein Units	4 oz (115 g) grilled chicken
1 Lo Vegetable Unit	1 mug cauliflower
1 Hi Vegetable Unit	1 medium jacket potato
	½ ear corn + 1
	*¾ mug skimmed milk

Add Daily

*2 Fruit Units	Indicated above with *
*1 Dairy Unit	Indicated above with *

         Women: 1–5 Flexi-Units (Core group only)
            Men: 5–8 Flexi-Units (Core group only)

WEEK TWO (B)

This is another example of Week Two. This time we have added 5 CORE Flexi-Units to the Core Diet. Count the + 1s; they add to 5.

CORE DIET	SAMPLE CORE MENU PLUS 5 Flexi-Units

Breakfast

1 Protein Unit	2 scrambled eggs + 1
1 Grain Unit	½ muffin, toasted
	*½ mug grapefruit juice

Lunch

3 Protein Units	3 oz (80 g) tuna, brine-packed
1 Grain Unit	1 oz (25 g) wholemeal bread
1 Lo Vegetable Unit	Lettuce
	1 tomato
	*1 plain yogurt

Dinner

4 Protein Units	4 oz (115 g) grilled chicken
1 Lo Vegetable Unit	1 mug cauliflower
1 Hi Vegetable Unit	½ mug peas
	⅓ mug tomato sauce + 1
	½ mug cooked pasta shells + 1
	*1 nectarine
	Coffee with cream + 1
	3 fl oz (80 ml) Chablis wine + 1

CORE DIET	SAMPLE CORE MENU PLUS 5 Flexi-Units

Add Daily

*2 Fruit Units	Indicated above with *
*1 Dairy Unit	Indicated above with *

Women: 1–5 Flexi-Units (Core group only)
Men: up to 8 Flexi-Units (Core group only)

WEEK THREE

Here is a sample of a Week Three plan as it contains CORE and MORE Flexi-Units for a total of 7. Note the 2 additional Flexi-Units of grilled or roast chicken in the dinner plan.

CORE DIET	SAMPLE CORE MENU PLUS 8 Flexi-Units (Core or More groups)

Breakfast

1 Protein Unit	1 scrambled egg
1 Grain Unit	1 oz (25 g) lean ham + 1
	1 whole muffin + 1
	*½ mug grapefruit juice

Lunch

3 Protein Units	3 oz (80 g) tuna, brine-packed
1 Grain Unit	1 oz (25 g) wholemeal bread
1 Lo Vegetable Unit	Lettuce
	1 mug cucumber and chopped celery
	*1 mug fresh fruit salad + 1
	*¼ mug whipped topping, non-dairy

DIETING SEVEN DAYS A WEEK: THE FLEXI-DIET

CORE DIET	SAMPLE CORE MENU PLUS 8 Flexi-Units (Core or More groups)
Dinner	
4 Protein Units 1 Lo Vegetable Unit 1 Hi Vegetable Unit	6 oz (170 g) roast chicken + 2 1 mug cauliflower 1 medium jacket potato 1 dinner roll, 1 oz (25 g) + 1
Snack	
	*1 mug skimmed milk 2 mugs popcorn + 1
Add Daily	
*2 Fruit Units *1 Dairy Unit	Indicated above with * Indicated above with *

Women: 1–5 Flexi-Units (Core and More group only)
Men: 5–8 Flexi-Units (Core and More group only)

Children and Teenagers

Children and teenagers have special needs, and the following recommended *additions* to The Core Diet are required for them each day.

Child age 6–12:
9 Flexi-Units to be chosen exactly as follows:
   3 Dairy Units
   1 Fruit Unit
   2 Grain Units
      plus
   3 Flexi-Units

Teenage boy 12–16
12 Flexi-Units to be chosen exactly as follows:
   3 Dairy Units
   3 Fruit Units
   1 Grain Unit
   2 Protein Units
      plus
   3 Flexi-Units

Teenage girl 12–16:
7 Flexi-Units to be chosen exactly as follows:
   2 Dairy Units
   2 Fruit Units
      plus
   3 Flexi-Units

Pregnancy And Nursing Mothers

Expectant mothers who are overweight should aim to maintain their weight unless their doctors advise them to lose weight during pregnancy. The Core Diet is the one most suited to them. Vitamin and mineral supplements should only be taken in pregnancy after consultation with the doctor.

The following additions to The Core Diet are recommended for them each day.

Pregnant and Breast Feeding Mothers:
7 Flexi-Units to be chosen exactly as follows:
   2 Dairy Units
   2 Fruit Units
      plus
   3 Flexi-Units

And Finally, Some Questions and Answers

Question: Can I stay on The Core Diet with no Flexi-Units added and lose weight more quickly?
Answer: Yes, but *only* for one week before adding Flexi-Units.

Minimal nutrition needs will be met by women eating no less than 1 Flexi-Unit, men no less than 5.

Question: Can I vary the number of Flexi-Units I eat each day?
Answer: Sure, follow The Flexi Diet any way you want; it's yours to design as you wish. Some people add fewer than their allowed Flexi-Units each day, Monday to Friday, and then eat their full daily allotment on Saturday and Sunday.

Question: I hate breakfast. Can I skip it and combine it with lunch?
Answer: Breakfast is an important meal. It gets you going for the day. We recommend eating three meals per day for optimal weight loss.

Question: I love a big breakfast. Can I combine it with lunch?
Answer: You can do better than that. We don't recommend combining a meal because that means you are skipping a meal, but you can use your Flexi-Units to eat as much protein, bread and fruit as you like for breakfast and then eat lunch.

Question: I hate chicken, and you have it listed every night for dinner on the sample menu plans.
Answer: These are *sample* menu plans only, to show you how the programme works. Choose any from the Protein Unit list that you like as a substitute.

Question: Can I mix my proteins and eat 2 Units of ham and 1 Unit of hard cheese for lunch?
Answer: Yes. You may mix and match your lunch Protein Units as you wish, provided that you don't exceed the recommended number of Units.

· CHAPTER ELEVEN ·

THE LAST TEN POUNDS PLUS BEST DIET TIPS

Just a few more pounds to go...

The last ten pounds are the hardest. At this point you've probably been on the diet for a while, and your motivation and morale may be at a low ebb.

It's true, too, that you are dealing here with fat that's been stuck on your body the longest, so it's the toughest to get off. After all, that fat has been compacted over time by more fat accumulation. No wonder it's stubborn and resistant.

We are going to deal with this old fat in a special and effective way. We're going to put your diet on a diet. And here's how.

When you are down to only ten pounds to go, cut your Wild Weekend Units in half. If you are a woman, permit yourself only 17 WWUs for the weekend, and if you are a man, allow yourself only 21.

What that means is that on Saturday night women will eat 11 WWUs, men will eat 14 WWUs. For Sunday lunch, women eat 6 WWUs, men 7.

This kind of dieting will boost your morale and your weight loss!

Best diet tips

By now you know a lot about The Wild Weekend Diet. But we've not finished yet. We will give you even more tools with which to succeed; we will give you our best diet tips. Here follow more than 100 helpful suggestions garnered from the world's most successful dieters and weight loss maintainers. You'll find these tips grouped into six major categories: Exercise; Self awareness; Behaviour Modification; Health; Stress Reduction; and Miscellaneous.

I don't expect you'll follow every last suggestion, nor do I expect you to try a whole bunch at one time. What I do expect is that you'll read them all. Then you will know that these aids are there for the time when you need the strength to diet one more day, because there will be those days. You will find them useful, also, when you are ready to become a Professional Eater.

A Professional Eater is a person who eats when and what she/he wants to eat and who keeps within goal range. Like any advanced activity, it takes time, effort and experience to become a professional.

Exercise tips

Many believe they cannot control the rate by which their bodies burn off fat. They think they're genetically predisposed, born, to burn fat at a set rate. Don't believe it – it's just not true. Simply stated, the more you move, the more you lose. Some experts believe that the benefits of exercising are long-lasting. They say that if you exercise briskly your body's metabolism will speed up and you'll continue burning calories at a faster rate for many hours after you've exercised.

Any exercise is better than none at all. Start with realistic goals, like walking to your lunch date instead of taking the car or bus, and build from there.

1. The best exercise is regular exercise. Don't force yourself to do conditioning exercises if you don't like them. Look instead for an activity you consider fun – swimming, tennis, golf, bicycling, long-distance walking, etc.

2. Choose an exercise that offers muscle strengthening and muscle flexing. Such exercises are: walking briskly at 3 miles an hour, jogging, skipping.

3. Always warm up before strenuous exercise. Stretch all your muscles and run or walk briskly in place until your heart rate increases. This will help you avoid any injury to 'cold', unstretched muscles.

4. Follow your workout with a 'cool down'. Do the same movements as in your warm-up. This will help you avoid the painful muscle tightening called cramps.

5. Start exercising gradually. Don't be one of those 'weekend athletes', starting out with a burst of enthusiasm on a Saturday morning and continuing with a 10-mile bike ride on Sunday. After not having been on a bicycle for 10 years, all that's going to happen with that strategy is that by Monday you'll be a bundle of aches and pains, with no further interest in physical fitness. So be smart. Start with walking. Walk briskly for 20 minutes three times a week. You can gradually increase the length of your walk, and then increase the frequency.

6. Don't overdo or underdo. It's quite natural to feel stretches and dull aches. However, if something hurts or gives you a sharp pain, stop.

7. Exercise at a pace at which you can carry on a normal conversation and not be short of breath.

8. Wear supportive, comfortable and well-fitting shoes. The greatest deterrent to successful exercise is sore feet. After exercising, baby your feet with a warm soak, cream or lotion, and a nice cool powdering all over. Then elevate them on a pillow and feel virtuous.

9. Don't exercise on an empty stomach. You don't ask your car to run without petrol. About 1–2 hours before your workout, have a light but nutritious meal. On the other hand, don't exercise on a full stomach. Allow time between your meal and exercise.

10. Exercising outdoors is truly invigorating. Try walking, golfing, tennis, swimming, bicycling, skiing, jogging, canoeing, running, mountain climbing.

11. Winter's no excuse for hibernation. Get an exercise bicycle or an adapator that will make your bike stationary for exercise in the house. Now you can fantasise about cycling anywhere in the world (without the typhoons and hurricanes) while warm and comfortable in your own home. More indoor exercises: mini-trampolines; table tennis; roller skating; ice skating; swimming; indoor tennis; dancing; or squash.

12. You don't need a partner to exercise. There's something to be said for a long walk by yourself. Take this time to reflect, to get acquainted with yourself – and to review your diet, making plans for the slim new you!

13. Get into the whole exercising thing – buy yourself a new exercise suit.

14. Think about buying a portable cassette player. Exercise is even better with music. Or take this time to play your foreign language tape. You might as well be slimming down while conjugating all those irregular verbs.

15. Don't get bored. Boredom is deadly. Vary your routine. Walk a different route, take a different companion, change your destination.

16. Wear a pedometer when you're walking to measure how far you've walked. See if you can beat your own record. Always look for chances to burn extra calories.

17. Carry the groceries to your car and then to your house.

18. Many people (who will remain nameless) accumulate piles at the bottom of the staircase. This is the I'll-take-them-all-up-later syndrome. Now, in the name of calorie burning, here is your big chance to reform. Take whatever it is up as soon as you can. This trip will be good for your soul – and your hips.

19. Go out for the newspapers yourself.

20. Take the dog for a walk instead of putting him out.

21. Ignore the lift or escalator; take the stairs. If you work on a top floor, walk to the second or third floor and catch the lift there.

22. Always walk *down* the stairs.

23. Park your car as far away as possible from your destination. Carry an umbrella in case of rain.

24. Use the following to learn how many calories you burn by doing your favourite exercise. You will be proud each time you finish your exercise and won't want to ruin its effects by eating. Remember, any exercise is better than no exercise.

ACTIVITY	WEIGHT*	CALORIES BURNED
Walking briskly	120 lb (54.4 kg)	308 per hour
Walking briskly	150 lb (68 kg)	401 per hour
Walking moderately	120 lb (54.4 kg)	163 per hour
Walking moderately	150 lb (68 kg)	213 per hour
Running	120 lb (54.4 kg)	500 per hour
Running	150 lb (68 kg)	651 per hour
Bicycling	120 lb (54.4 kg)	233 per hour
Bicycling	150 lb (68 kg)	304 per hour
Swimming	120 lb (54.4 kg)	180 per hour
Swimming	150 lb (68 kg)	235 per hour
Skipping	120 lb (54.4 kg)	388 per hour
Skipping	150 lb (68 kg)	420 per hour

* Body weight influences the number of calories burned. The heavier the body weight, the more energy expended in exercising.

MORE CALORIE/ACTIVITY INFORMATION

Less than 1 calorie/minute:

Sleeping, lying down

1–2 calories/minute:

Sitting: reading, handwork, crafts, card playing, listening to music, eating, talking, typing, using business machines

2–3 calories/minute:

Standing up: telephoning, cooking, stand-up crafts
Self care: washing face, showering, shaving, setting hair
Light housekeeping: sweeping, dusting, picking up
Simple calisthenics and casual exercise, badminton

3–5 calories/minute:

Brisk walking
Shopping
Washing car
Heavy housework: scrubbing floor, washing windows, making beds, vacuuming, ironing
Sports: bowling, dancing, exercising

More than 5 calories/minute:

Walking up and down stairs
Mowing with handmower
Snow shovelling
Outdoor gardening
Jogging and running
Very active calisthenics: fast push-ups, skipping
Tennis match
High-speed bicycling
Skiing
Active dancing
Steady swimming
Brisk game of golf

Self awareness

One of the keys to successful weight loss is to be aware of the pitfalls you'll encounter in losing weight. Each of us has his or her own stumbling block. The following tips will help you on the WSP, that straight and narrow road between Wild Weekends.

1. Food is lovely, as we all agree. But if it's always been your reward, find another. A scarf, a book, a ticket to the match, anything you can't eat.

2. Start a hobby, preferably something that keeps your hands busy and your mind off the refrigerator.

3. Don't test your willpower. If it were great you wouldn't be dieting.

4. Resist the urge to weigh yourself frequently. On The Wild Weekend Diet weigh yourself only once a week on a regular schedule. When you reach your goal, you can weigh yourself more often.

5. Get involved with activities that keep your morale high. It's easier to diet when you feel good about yourself.

6. During the week, keep no junk food in the house! The Wild Weekend is coming. Indulge yourself *then*, and not before.

7. If you want to snack between meals, take fruit, coke, or a small green salad.

8. If you live alone, you've got an advantage. There is no reason to have problem foods in the house. On the other hand, you may be tempted to skip regular meals altogether and snack all day. Don't. The nutritional cost is too high.

9. Don't feel obliged to hide the fact that you're dieting. You have the right to try to be your best and healthiest self. Remember, when worrying about the opinion of others, they do not live in your body. You do.

10. Eat three meals daily. Skipping breakfast and lunch only sets you up for an apocalypse at the dinner table and beyond.

11. Forget guilt. One goof does not a disaster make. You're not the first person to fall off the wagon. Just get back on it, like all the rest of us who are now slim.

12. Remember with the next mouthful that you are back on The Wild Weekend Diet.

13. Keep a diet diary. It's amazing how much food we all eat and then completely forget. Write down everything you eat every day for at least three weeks. Even broken biscuits count!

14. Keep track of all the foods you resisted during the week. It will soon be evident to you how many calories you used to eat. Then boast to yourself about how strong and controlled you are about food.

15. Use awareness techniques. When your mind whispers 'food' to you, lift up your hand and turn off that switch.

16. At the same time click your mind on to foodless pictures – an exotic foreign scene, a bubble bath, a new book, a phone call. Act on your mental picture.

17. Write yourself a letter and say goodbye to your fat. List every reason to hate the fat on your body, why it keeps you from doing what you want to do, keeps you from being who you want to be. Mail the letter and read it every time you want to over-eat.

18. Find a picture of yourself when you were thin. You've never been thin? Okay, then cut out a picture of someone who now looks as you want to look. Then paste your face on that person's body. Put this picture where you can see it frequently during the day and during the evening, or put it next to your alarm clock so that it is the first thing you see every morning and the last thing you see every night. Say to yourself, 'That's me!'

19. As you lose pounds and inches your clothes become too big for you. Tailor them down to your new size or get rid of them. If you know you have only clothes that fit, you'll have one more reason to stay thin.

20. If you are not working and don't wish to, find a voluntary organisation that will expand your horizons. Expend some concern on others, not your stomach.

21. Don't be disappointed when others do not praise you for your weight loss. Some people are openly hostile to good losers because they cannot stand success of any kind in others. Remember always that you are conquering yourself. You can do anything!

22. Identify your weakness. If you eat because you are bored, start a new hobby. If you eat because you are lonely, join a club or dig out your library card and read, read, read. If you eat because you are happy, tell yourself how much happier you'd be if you were thinner. If it's anger or depression that brings the hand to mouth, work out these emotions in a better way. Exercise, talk with a friend, see a

counsellor, or take a walk to a quiet, scenic place. Or scrub the floor or fix the back door step. Do anything else, but don't eat your anger and depression. It will only eat you.

23. Study calories. If you learn that your favourite binge is 100 calories plus, some of the lure of that food will vanish.

Behaviour modification

Behaviour modification, as it relates to weight loss, is the science of changing fat and negative thoughts and actions to thin and positive thoughts and actions. Most of us have spent a lifetime learning to be fat. The following tips will help you learn to be thin.

1. Practise eating as a solitary act. Eat your meals without watching television or reading the newspaper or a magazine. Concentrate on your food and savour every bite. Often when you are distracted while eating you don't experience the enjoyment of your food and you may go looking for more.

2. Eat sitting down. And only in a proper place, such as at the kitchen or dining room table, at the picnic table or on a blanket or in a restaurant or in a pub. When you stop giving yourself permission to eat standing up, you have removed a frequent cause of mis-eating.

3. Stop eating when your body tells you it is satisfied. Push your plate away and throw out the leftovers. If picking at the leftover food on your plate is a problem, and you can't immediately throw it away, sprinkle pepper or salt or sugar all over it.

4. Have only low calorie beverages between meals. Practise the art of eating only during mealtimes.

5. Keep a journal of your feelings about dieting. Write down any frustrations you may have, and get rid of them by writing instead of eating. Also, record how good you feel

while dieting. This will help you stick with your positive eating plan.

6. Use smaller plates to serve your food. Servings will look larger then. Deceive your eyes; you cannot con the scales.

7. Eat one mouthful of food at a time. Chew each bite thoroughly and swallow it before taking the next bite. This helps you eat more slowly and thereby fill up faster.

8. You do have control over food. Prove it by leaving some on the plate. Say no and mean it.

9. Eat slowly and consciously. Try eating with chopsticks or baby utensils or your opposite hand. These activities help you concentrate on eating and make the act of eating less automatic.

10. Put a standing mirror on your table and watch yourself eat. Many people are totally unaware of their rapid eating habits until they see themselves shovelling in the food. Pretend you are dining with a film star, and as you eat, act chic, poised and unhurried.

11. Stop and mentally ask yourself for permission to eat before you start. This is probably the most important of all behaviour changes. When you learn not to eat what you do not need, you've won a victory over your fat.

12. Keep a record of people or situations that trigger the wrong eating habits. Make a list of the 'binge' foods. You can control it by staying away from it. Same goes for people. You can still enjoy these people's company but not for lunch or dinner.

13. Eat only what you've planned in advance. Make out a week's menu and stick to it. Make no change or substitutions. Fill out your menu after you have eaten and then make a shopping list from your menu.

14. Shop by list only. Make a weekly shopping list at home. Go through your cupboards and refrigerator to see what you

need. When you get to the supermarket, buy only the foods on your list and take only enough cash with you for them. If this fails, send someone else to the shop for you and tell them to buy only what you've listed.

15. Put your fork down between bites. Repeat the procedure to eat only one mouthful at a time, then add to it by putting down your fork before taking the next bite. Take at least twenty minutes to eat your meals.

16. Enlist the support of your family and friends. Tell them you are dieting, and ask them to please give you a break and refrain from urging you to eat what you shouldn't.

17. Tell yourself that you will diet 100 per cent this week. Promise yourself a perfect five days on the WSP. Each time you feel tempted to go off, tell yourself The Wild Weekend is coming.

18. Make out a personal reward list. Write down any and all gifts, pleasures and activities you like. Then plan to select one reward at least three or four times per week. Being rewarded for making a change in behaviour makes changing easier and more exciting.

19. Cook a new recipe each week. Try all of the WSP recipes in Chapter 4 at least once, and create your own, following the WSP cooking guidelines.

20. Exercise daily. Refer to the tips on exercise earlier in this chapter and get moving! While you are exercising you cannot eat.

21. Tell yourself three good things about yourself and your life each day. Build up your confidence and begin to appreciate how special and wonderful you really are. Tell yourself this over and over again until you believe it. You should believe it; it's true.

Health

Good health is precious – a birthright. But good health doesn't just fall your way; you can help yourself to better health by following these tips.

1. Sleep. Most of us require seven to eight hours of sleep per night to give the body the rest it needs to repair itself from the stress of the day. Be sure you get just the right amount of sleep your body requires. Too much or too little is not healthy.

2. Rest. This is different from sleep. Rest is the act of shutting everything down, if only for a few moments. Stare out of the window and daydream for five or ten minutes. Close your office or bedroom door, prop up your feet, put your head back, and take several deep breaths before resuming your schedule. Take a fifteen-minute catnap – put your head down on the desk or table and let your weary mind wander. Set a clock if you tend to fall into a deep sleep.

3. Relax. Again, this is different from sleep and rest. You can relax in any situation. Even if you are in the middle of a board meeting or stuck in traffic, breathe deeply and regularly and tighten all your muscle groups, one group at a time, then relax them. You will feel refreshed and ready to go back to your activity.

4. Exercise. We've talked a lot in this chapter about the role of exercise in weight control. Exercise is vital to good health, and there's not a lot more to say about it except do it!

5. Take vitamins and mineral supplements, regardless of how little or how much you eat. Today's food supply does not contain the nutrients that were present in the foods your parents or grandparents ate. The soil is depleted. The environment wreaks havoc with nutrients. Modern food-processing techniques rob food of its nutrients, then food storage, transportation and cooking deplete nutrients further. Good health is more assured by supplementing your everyday diet with vitamins and minerals.

6. Pleasure. Remember 'All work and no play makes Jack a dull boy'? It's true. And our life in the fast lane often leaves little room for fun and pleasure. Make room. You owe it to your body and soul.

7. Eat good food. On The Wild Weekend Diet you have the foods of the world from which to choose. Make each choice a healthy choice. Make sure you're getting good nutrition in return for all the calories you are spending.

8. Reduce salt, sugar and fat. The less of these you take in, the thinner and healthier you will be.

9. Check your blood pressure regularly. This is one illnesss that definitely can be controlled. If you don't have high blood pressure, practising good health measures will probably help you avoid it altogether.

10. Drink plenty of water. Water helps you feel less hungry, and it also washes out the body's impurities. Drink six to eight cups of pure water daily. Bottled water and spring water are good alternatives to tea, coffee, or diet drinks.

11. Reduce your intake of alcohol and stop smoking. Take medications only as prescribed by your physician. Weight loss, good health, plenty of rest, relaxation and exercise will surely lessen your frequency of trips to the doctor and your need for medications.

Stress reduction

Stress is being pulled in more than one direction at once. It is positive as well as negative. Positive stress gives you an incentive to achieve good things. Stress is negative only when it is excessive. Too much stress is hazardous to your diet, your health and your life.

The time clock, the executive meeting, the rude customer, the screaming boss, bumper-to-bumper traffic, the road hogs, the stuck horn, the doctor's surgery, the dentist's drill, demanding children, losing your job, marriage, divorce, exams, birth of a new baby, loss of a loved one – these events in our lives, pleasant and unpleasant, cause stress. Routine is stress. You cannot escape stress, but you can learn to live with it.

To reduce the harmful effects of stress in your life, follow these tips.

1. Avoid friction. Keep away from people and situations that cause you discomfort. You do not need unnecessary worry, concern, frustration or grief.

2. Deal with difficulties head-on. In other words, stop procrastinating. Some people spend money or waste hours agonising about doing something they don't want to do or have a hard time doing. The problem, therefore, is always present, causing unnecessary stress. Do the hard things first in your day, and then the rest of the day will be 'easier'.

3. Exercise. Here it is again! Exercise reduces stress immensely. Clear your mind as you move all your muscles. Exercise rids your body of excess adrenaline caused by stress. Afterwards you'll be relaxed, with an inner calmness and a better ability to deal with day-to-day problems. Exercise helps you function mentally much more efficiently. The best way to relax the mind is to move the legs.

4. Create a relaxing environment. Dim the lights and shut out noise. Close your eyes and practise deep, normal breathing. Slowly go through, one at a time, all the muscle groups in your body, tighten them, hold them, then relax them. Start with your feet, then your calves, then thighs, then buttocks, then abdomen, then chest and shoulder area, then upper arms, lower arms, hands, neck, and finally the face muscles. Then go back to see if you still feel any tense areas in your body. If you do, tighten those muscles again and relax them. Repeat this until all the tension in your body is gone. You will feel very relaxed and the physical stress will be gone.

5. Follow The Wild Weekend Diet or the Flexi Diet plans. Being well nourished helps you to handle stress best.

6. Listen to soothing music. Sit down and put on an easy-listening record or tape.

7. Get a massage or learn to give yourself one. It is one of the best relaxers.

8. Change What You Can – Accept What You Cannot – Have the Wisdom to Know the Difference.

Miscellaneous

And, finally, here are a few more tips to help you realise your goal of being thinner!

1. Give yourself time to lose weight. You didn't get fat overnight and you won't get back to where you want to be overnight! A healthy average weight loss for women is 1–2 pounds (½–1 kg) per week after the first week. If a 1–2 pound loss is discouraging, imagine 1–2 pounds of hamburger sticking over each of your hips. And ask yourself, 'Do I want that back?'

2. When you think you're beaten, you aren't. So, don't give up! Giving up is easy. Getting on with it isn't. But remember, at any point in your diet you are further ahead than when you began. Keep on going. Remember, 'Quitters Never Win and Winners Never Quit!'

3. Life is a battle. So is dieting. Arm yourself for battles. If you know the party you are going to may offer too many temptations, be ready for it. Start telling yourself five days before that you will not over-eat. Write this thought down. Believe it. Picture yourself at that party and not over-eating. Rehearse this scene over and over again. When you do go to the party, your not over-eating behaviour will be natural.

4. Jazz yourself up. You're eating good food, shedding fat and changing on the inside. Do something for your outside. Try a new chic hairstyle, get a manicure, have a professional

make-up (you can get one free at many department stores), colour your hair, or buy dazzling, outrageous clothing accessories. Decorate yourself, not a cake.

5. Take your measurements daily. Often weight loss is shown faster this way, and you will be rewarded quickly. A quarter of an inch (6 mm) off the waist is a great loss.

6. Make another list. Call it 'How to Stay Fat'. Write down every example you can think of, such as: picking at food while I cook; buying fattening goodies (in case friends drop in); and riding when I can walk, etc. Then eliminate each of these habits one by one. You'll be on your way to eliminating fat at the same time.

7. Make contracts with family and friends. Ask your family to perform tasks in the kitchen that might cause you to mis-eat. In exchange you can offer to hire a video for the weekend. Ask friends and co-workers to keep the sweets out of your environment, and in turn offer to do something for them. This works.

8. Change what you feed others. If you believe it's important to your health to avoid foods with empty (non-nutritious) calories, then it's important to the health of those you care about, too. Change your way of thinking when planning meals. The side benefit to you, of course, is that the food won't be around to tempt you.

9. When it comes to holiday planning, place your emphasis on the true meaning of the holiday at hand. Then plan activities to support this. Make the meal planning secondary. Consider food at the time to be necessary to well-being but not the reason for the celebration.

10. Become a proponent of 'coffee and conversation'. One successful dieter we know told the story of being invited to a neighbour's house for coffee. She was served her coffee and kept waiting for the 'and'. It never came. She left that neighbour's house feeling insulted. Guess: Was the neighbour fat or thin? She was *thin*! Today our dieter is also thin,

and when she invites someone for coffee, that's all she serves.

11. Eliminate such diet-breaking excuses from your vocabulary as 'The devil made me do it', 'I carry my weight well', 'Broken biscuits don't count', 'My husband likes women to look like women'. Instead, add to your vocabulary: 'There is no reason why I couldn't be thinner and healthier.'

12. Surround yourself with your best friends: a full-length mirror, weighing scales and tape measure, cucumber, celery and slices of green and red peppers, The Wild Weekend Diet, and a cobra in your fridge!

13. Practise the dieter's exercises of placing both of your hands on the edge of the table and pushing away. Shake your head from left to right, often. Reach for your mate instead of your plate. Run past the cake shop.

14. Remember the dieting rewards: flowers, escape weekends, health-club memberships, facials, massages, stereo radios with headphones.

15. Fat-proof your environment. Get the biscuits out of the clothes hamper. Remove the chocolates from the lingerie drawer. Take the sweets out of your desk and the crisps out of your glove compartment. Put marbles in the bon bon dish (or coloured soaps or pretty seashells). Put a piranha in the biscuit jar.

16. Take your diet one day at a time. Learn all that you can about yourself and make small changes one at a time. This way you won't feel discouraged, and you will go further in your success than you ever imagined!

17. When you eat or drink naked foods (not mixed with Hot List items or prepared according to the Hot List methods), your dieting will go best.

18. Paper your house, your desk, you car, and the cat with memos. Make a copy of each of the following statements

and put them where you will see them every day, many times a day.

- Temptations only come in the door you leave open.
- The best meal lasts but a few hours. Thin lasts forever.
- Feeling good is wearing your shirt tucked in.
- Don't watch your weight, lose it!
- What you eat in private shows up in public.
- If you learned to be fat, you can learn to be thin.
- Think thin! Act thin! Be thin!

· CHAPTER TWELVE ·

MAINTENANCE AND A NEW BEGINNING

A time to turn

One of the most interesting circumstances of life is change. You have lost your weight and you are a success. In achieving a weight-loss goal you've made a change, a change in your appearance, and perhaps a change because you allowed yourself to be successful. For many people significant weight loss is the first real success in their lives. Perhaps this is true for you.

Whether this is your first success, or one of many, you face a new question: You have been a successful amateur – now what?

You pulled it off, you saw it through; you lost weight, and it wasn't easy – it never is – but you did it. What do you do for an encore? You can't ride on the crest of that dieting success for ever. We all need new goals to work for. In your case the goal is maintenance – to stay slim for ever you must turn professional.

A new beginning

There is a story told about the founder of judo. As you may know, judo, like all martial arts, marks success and progression by the colour of belts. The beginners are given a white belt, and through a series of steps and achievements, they may work their way up to a black belt. The black belt proclaims to you and to the world that you are a master with the skill, the dedication, the discipline, and the perseverance to achieve on the highest level.

One day, as the founder of judo lay very old and ill in bed, a disciple came to him and asked that he share the secrets of his expertise with his followers. The founder agreed to do this and expressed his secret in a single thought: Each time you attempt a new step, seek a new level, choose a new goal requiring new techniques, a new discipline, you must put on your white belt anew and begin again at the beginning.

Each of you has, to a greater or lesser degree, struggled to achieve your goal-range weight. You will find that maintaining this weight loss is a new challenge and requires a new struggle.

Consider yourself an expert at dieting and a novice at maintenance. Award yourself the black belt for having achieved success, and then put your white belt on and learn how to maintain that weight loss.

You have a new goal but the same needs. Recognise that you must begin again. Your objective is different, but the vigilance and discipline needed are the same. As before, you need information, techniques and motivation to maintain your weight loss.

The second decision

Losing weight required a decision on your part. You made that decision and you lost weight. Now you must make a second decision – to be thin for ever. And just as you took the time and effort to learn about a diet and behaviours that ensured your personal weight loss, so, too, must you come up with a personal maintenance package that is right for you. For most of us, maintaining is more challenging and frustrating than dieting. Dieting is difficult, but it is also very simple. When you subtract calories from your intake, you subtract pounds from your body, and eventually the job is done; you're within goal range. By the time you've got down to where you want to be you have a good idea of what you have to do to burn up the fat. Maintenance is not so simple; on maintenance you must write your own script.

Keeping it off

If you had any hope of going back to your old style of eating now that you are at your goal, abandon that hope. Listen to your inner voice of reason as it tells you that if you go back to your old style of eating you'll go back to your old, fat figure as well.

As during the weight-loss process, on maintenance, ignorance is not bliss. It is disaster. Some things you must know.

Calories

You must know how many calories you burn up each day. Many women do not believe that 3,500 calories equal a pound. Some women believe that they gain weight by simply *smelling* the wrappers that contain food. Not a fact. Smelling does not put on pounds. Neither does looking. Eating does. So what holds true for women is that they burn from 11 to 12 calories per pound of their ideal weight each day. For men this number varies between 14 and 17. Men are, in general, larger than women, weigh more and, consequently, they get to eat more without the penalty of weight gain.

To work out the approximate number of calories to maintain weight loss for a woman who is 115 pounds, we multiply 115 by 12, which gives us 1,380 calories per day, or 9,660 a week. To figure the approximate number of calories for a man to maintain, let's multiply 160 by 15, which gives him 2,400 calories per day or 16,800 per week.

Weight

You also need to know how much you weigh over a week's time. It is impossible to maintain an absolute weight on a day-to-day basis. It is possible, however, and most practical, to stay within that Goal Range most of the time.

The weighing scale is the instrument you will use to measure your status. It is an equal partner to your eating plan in the maintenance process. You have to pledge that you will trust the information your instrument gives you. Keep informed regularly. Preferably daily. Not less than weekly.

The great weight maintenance experiments

You've reached your goal weight. And now comes a time of testing. What can you eat? Anything? How much? The following are three experiments to give you a start on your own maintenance scriptwriting. These have been helpful to many. But maintenance is an individual matter, so you may wish to alter any given plan so that it makes sense in your life.

One experiment of maintenance is to stay on the diet that worked for you before and add foods each day within a calorie limit or by units. A variation of that theme for Wild Weekend Dieters would be to increase Wild Weekend Units on Saturday and Sunday and stay on the Weekday Slimdown Plan during the week. Or The Core Diet. The WSP is a menu expression of The Core Diet.

A second experiment calls for you to set a calorie limit for each day and to just stop eating when you reach that limit. This works for many people. A variation of this theme is to keep track of calories and keep them low during the week and have a 'free' weekend.

Or you may want to try a combination of the experiments above and keep your calories very low from Monday to Friday. Give yourself the weekends 'free', with no thought to calories or to Wild Weekend Units.

As frustrating and anxiety-provoking as this experimenting may be, it is a necessary information-gathering step so that you can establish the food and situational limits for your thin future. You can do it! You have already established through your initial weight loss that you have strength and resolve.

The length of this testing phase is not fixed by the calendar. Diet arithmetic is frustrating; it doesn't add up or subtract down to anything that might resemble a precise schedule. You may learn what you need to know in six months, or it may take you two years. You know it's over when you experience the relief from anxiety around food and eating that comes from knowing exactly what you have to do to be thin for ever and that you have made peace with those limits. You have also come to the realisation that food is not a treat that you give yourself; it is the fuel your body needs to keep going. You will have to think carefully about the following:

- Which foods and drinks are really important to you?

- Are there some foods that come with such a high calorie price tag that they're not worth the purchase?
- Do you know which foods trigger mis-eating for you?

No one is perfect

As you progress with your experiments and expand your food limits, you may come to a difficult phase. Without warning, bad eating habits, poor control and thoughtless behaviour make an appearance, and unexpected weight gains show on the scales.

It is an important part of the long-term success process for you to give yourself permission to be imperfect. You didn't become a Diet Angel when you lost your weight; no one is. Angels don't have to diet. We do. And occasionally we all slip. We take the easy way — like eating the butter on the fish we ordered dry, or eating more than we intended to, or eating something we didn't really want or didn't plan for.

When you mis-eat without thought, reflect back on this incident. Replay and analyse it. What caused it? There's always a reason. You can depend on this. Decide what you will do next time you are in a similar situation. Write yourself a new ending to the scene. This time stay in control; this time you win. Then congratulate yourself for being able to do the replay because it is this kind of attention, this kind of discipline that saw you through the weight-loss process and this is now insurance for your thin future.

Tips to keep you thin

- Keep foods that are hard for you to handle out of your house. You don't need to be a pillar of willpower; you need to be thin.

- Work those foods and drinks that are really important to you into your personal maintenance plan.

- Exercise does burn up calories. Consider adding movement to your life.

- Learn the calorie content of the foods you especially like to eat often.
- Keep a food diary.
- Keep a weight chart.
- Emphasise the sociability aspect of eating out and of parties rather than the food.
- Give away your fat clothes. Or burn them. Getting rid of them is a must.
- Dress for the new you. Toss out old, dull clothes.
- Change your hairstyle and, if you're a woman, your make-up.
- Invest the energy that you had for dieting in a new interest.
- Keep a journal and record the feelings you're experiencing about food and eating.

As you buckle on your white belt to begin again on thinness maintenance, remember that you are not really back to the beginning. For each time you start again, you bring to the new experience information about yourself and about the subject; in this case, healthy eating and weight loss, and you bring your success experience.

As you set out on your thin life remind yourself frequently that you have acomplished something important and valuable for yourself. Something difficult. Give yourself full credit. You are a black belt, an achiever on the highest level of skill.